Fred Myers Chronicles

Life Adventures and Real Cases
Told by a Diligent Detective

Fred Myers Chronicles

Life Adventures and Real Cases
Told by a Diligent Detective

Volume I
A Case for the Kids

FRED MYERS

WITH MAJOR CONTRIBUTIONS BY KAY MYERS

EXPERT PRESS

Fred Myers Chronicles
Life Adventures and Real Cases Told by a Diligent Detective

Volume I: A Case for the Kids

© 2021 Fred Myers

ISBN-13: 978-1-946203-87-8

The stories described within are factual; some names and circumstances have been changed to preserve the privacy of those involved.

www.ExpertPress.net

Acknowledgment

Although my name, Fred Myers, may be on the front of this book, it is not just my story. This story would not be possible without my wonderful wife, Kay. Kay and I have been partners in life for over sixty years, and it is because of her I was able to build the investigation business and travel the world recovering children and working other cases. She has always put our family first and has always seen to every need and want. She was the neighborhood mom who had get-togethers for the kids and their friends, as well as huge parties and reunions for our friends and families. She has always gone out of her way to make our home life very special and full and has always taken care of everyone else.

If taking care of me and our five children was not enough, Kay worked in our business from the very beginning. She helped with marketing, clerical work, operating switchboards, and she served as a licensed private investigator and a server of legal process papers for many years. She was the most successful process server the business ever had, and she had a special knack for getting information from people who otherwise would not have provided it. Kay would always feed the investigators when they would show up at our home unannounced at dinner time; she always makes sure everyone feels welcome and loved. Kay has filled my life and our children's lives with love and laughter, and I am forever grateful for her.

Both Kay's and my family background and upbringing and our love and experiences with our foster children as well as our own five children shaped our desire, our ability, and our willingness to take the risks we did for the children in this story.

The eighty-four years God has given me to live thus far have been full, rich and blessed. I have spent sixty-two years with my one love, Kay, and together we built a beautiful family that includes five children and their spouses and eight grandchildren.

I thank God my Lord and Savior, Jesus Christ, for all His blessings throughout my life. He has showered me with many blessings including peace in my heart while I am alive and in eternal life in Heaven when I leave this world — who could ask for more?

My greatest hope and prayer is a continuation of one my mother prayed and that is, after this life is over for all of us, the family circle in Heaven will be unbroken and that we will all be together for eternity. That will be my greatest blessing.

Mr. and Mrs. Fred Myers
Nov. 1, 1958

Contents

Prologue

"No, Mr. Myers, you are not free to go."

My heart sank. These were not the words I wanted to hear at the end of these last anxious weeks and months. I was more than 6,000 miles from my Little Rock home, in the middle of Libya, an unstable country hostile to the United States.

All I could think of was my family—my wife Kay and our four young children—at home in Arkansas anxiously awaiting my return. Suddenly I wasn't sure if I would even see them again.

It was one of those moments when your whole life flashes before your eyes. How did I, Fred Myers from Arkansas, end up in such dire straits?

In a strange way, my entire life's journey had led me to this moment. It was the faith, values, and work ethic instilled by my parents. It was the love of my wife and children. It was the experience I had gained from a wide variety of jobs. It was my own constant hunger for learning and for new experiences. I had taken all those elements and forged my own path as a private investigator, and that unlikely path had somehow led me to this terrifying time and place.

How did I get there? Let me tell you …

Chapter 1

The Early Years

ON OCT. 29, 1936, I, Fred Myers, was born in a small sharecropper's house on a rural farm southwest of Warren, Arkansas. The location of my birthplace is roughly five miles south of the Ebenezer Cemetery where my mother, father, and many other relatives from generations prior now rest. I was named Fredrick Monroe Myers and nicknamed "Freddy" by family and friends as I grew older. This nickname matured to "Fred" after I graduated from high school and entered the Army.

My father, Homer Lee Myers, was born on Dec. 20, 1893 in Drew County, south of Monticello, Arkansas, in the Lacy community. He taught himself piano and violin around the age of ten, and then he proceeded to learn an array of other musical instruments throughout his lifetime. He was an amazing musician.

As I grew up, on many weekend evenings our home would be overflowing with visitors who would come to hear my father play whatever musical instrument he had. He taught others how to play instruments, including the Bryant Boys, who still play today. My father adored music and would play at anyone's request.

My father was drafted into the Army in 1917 and served during World War I for three years, with one of those years being in Germany. While there, he acquired a used violin with the words "Joseph Stradivarius" burned into the inside wood. This violin is still in our family today, over a century later. He never had its authenticity verified, nor did he ever have it appraised. His explanation was that he did not wish to sell it at any price. He just wanted to play it.

After his discharge from the Army, my father worked as a farmer, carpenter, a part-time barber, and was a country preacher, serving as a "fill-in" preacher whenever a church in the area was in need of one.

He became a preacher in 1940 after announcing to our church at the time that he had been called by God to preach. He studied the Bible and attended every church function he could to learn and contribute. He became a cherished preacher who would regularly fill in at several churches in the Freewill Baptist denomination. He was scheduled to preach at a church near Warren, Arkansas, on a Sunday morning in March 1960, when he passed from a heart attack at 66 years old.

His father — my grandfather — was also a farmer and country preacher. I was named after him. My grandmother, Laura Myers, was an amazing and respected woman who was a teacher and excellent singer. She passed in 1940 when she was living with my immediate family. I still remember some of the stories she told me; telling stories was one part of our family entertainment back then.

There is one story I remember in particular: One night, around 1900, when her children were small, she heard dogs fighting in her front yard. My grandfather was not home, so my grandmother ran onto the porch with a broom in hand and struck the rear of what she thought was a large yellow dog attacking the family dogs. The animal turned quickly to face her, showing itself to be a snarling panther. Before she could escape, the panther leapt on to the roof of the porch. She was determined to stay out of the dogs' potential fights after that!

My mother, known as Lena to her friends and Ms. Lena to the younger community near Warren, was born on Aug. 7, 1903. She was born in the Pleasant Valley community, about five miles south of where I was born. She met my father at a revival at the Pleasant Valley Freewill Baptist Church where her father, Dory Howsen, was an elder and a deacon. She married my father on Nov. 14, 1920, when she was only 17. I was born when she was 33 years old; I was her ninth child. The farm where I was born was known as the "Suzie Hariston Place." As far as I understand, one of Suzie's sons still lives on that farm today.

All of my mother's children were born at home with the attendants being a midwife from the community or Dr. Armstrong from Hermitage, Arkansas. The doctor would sometimes arrive after the baby had already been born but would check on health of my mother and the new baby. He took his pay in the form of a pig or a couple of chickens taking them home with him in his old Model-T.

We moved frequently when I was a small boy. The winter I was born we moved to England, Arkansas, where my father sharecropped for another farmer the next year. The next winter, we moved to the community of Macedonia, onto the Martin Place, located between Warren and New Edinburg. This is where my younger brother Cecil was born on Feb. 16, 1939. I still remember the morning I found out about his birth. The night before, the smaller of us children were sent down the road to Mr. and Mrs. Sanders. The next morning, my older sister Grachel walked us home while telling us about our new baby brother. She was 15 at the time, I was almost two and a half.

We lived on the Martin Place for about three years and sharecropped Mr. Martin's farmland. Sharecropping was done by arrangement with the landowner. The sharecropper would farm the land, then split the profit from crops grown on that land 50-50 with the owner. Mr. Martin furnished the land, provided all farm animals, equipment, and money to invest back into the farm by seeds, fertilizer, et cetera. We lived in a house owned by Mr. Martin and provided the labor to prepare the land, tend the crops and sell them.

Mr. Martin was adored by most of his neighbors and he treated us very well. We received better treatment through him than how many other sharecroppers were treated. He shared his milk cows, fruit trees, and other amenities with us. He was a widower who lived alone, so my mother provided him with many meals throughout our time there. He responded with kindness to our family.

My grandmother, as previously mentioned, lived with us for a year before she passed. She would keep Cecil, my older brother Victor, and me while my family worked in the field. Our only heat in the home was an open fireplace and a wood-burning cook stove. I remember one day I tossed some string into that fireplace. When the string caught fire, it traveled and caused my pants to ignite! My grandmother chased and caught me, then fell on me to put the fire out.

My grandmother passed at 80 years old due to heart failure. She is buried in a cemetery near Lacy, Arkansas, next to her first husband.

I have fond memories of my time at Martin's Place. One day, my brother Bill went to an old house nearby to draw water from a well for Mr. Martin's cattle. My siblings Mildred, Nina, Victor, and myself tagged along. We saw there was another old abandoned well nearby. The wooden curb was rotted off at ground level. My siblings and I were peering down into the darkness of the well. My feet began to slip, and I found myself falling into the well. I quickly threw out my arms to catch the old rotten curb. I was dangling by my hands into what could have possibly been my death. My siblings grabbed a hold of my arms, and my brother Bill came over to pull me to safety. This type of near-miss was commonplace; we kids had to look out for each other.

While at the Martin Place, we bought two very important items that our family extensively used throughout my growing years. One was a Singer sewing machine that my mother was so extremely proud of. Prior to the machine, she was hand sewing my family's clothes. We also purchased a battery-powered radio as we did not have electricity in our home; that radio provided us with information throughout World War II.

My brother Austin married his wife Geneva while we were living at the Martin Place. He was 19; she was 15. They were together for over 75 years and raised nine children before Austin passed away at age 96.

We moved from the Martin Place to the Thompson Place, about five miles away, in 1941. We lived there for a year and sharecropped with Mr. Thompson, who had a son named Billy Thompson that Victor and I played with. Billy and his wife remained close friends for years to my older brother Austin and Austin's wife, Geneva.

The fall of 1941, I entered my first year of school at New Edinburg, Arkansas. I was five years old and starting the first grade. This year was the year my grandfather Howsen passed as well as the start of World War II and the bombing of Pearl Harbor.

My family moved to the Ballentine Place in 1942. We lived there for around a year. My father began to work for the Works Progress Administration where he did carpentry work. We then proceeded to move to a small house owned by Mr. Charlie

Parker, my brother Austin's father-in-law. A short time after we had moved in, the house caught fire and the roof was severely damaged. I remember neighbors forming a water chain, passing buckets of water from person to person to fight the fire.

Austin was drafted into the Navy in early 1942. My brother Doyle enlisted a few months later; however, our father had to sign an authorization for Doyle to enlist. Both, upon completion of basic training, were assigned to separate ships in the South Pacific. They were involved in several battles throughout the war but did not see each other for nearly three years. My sister Grachel attempted to enlist in the Women Accepted for Volunteer Emergency Service program but was rejected because she was too small. She then enlisted in the Women's Army Corp and was accepted.

In August 1945, three and a half years after the Pearl Harbor bombing, as the war was winding down, thousands of ships from several fleets were docked in and around the Bay of Tokyo. Doyle was on the flagship of the Fifth Fleet as ships were docking. He used his binoculars and, as fate would have it, spotted his brother's ship anchored nearby. He immediately notified his commander and requested radio contact be made to see if Austin was on the ship. It was confirmed, and Doyle's commander supplied him with a small boat to board Austin's ship. Austin was completely flabbergasted at his brother's appearance on his ship! They were fortunate to spend four hours together at a safe location on a nearby shore, as they did not see each other again until the war was over and they came home

During the war, we moved to another house Mr. Parker owned that was next to the Macedonia Freewill Baptist Church. It was a four-room wood frame house with an outhouse and a chicken coop. There were eight of us living in that house.

We had moved again in 1944 to the Eb White Place at the intersection of the New Edinburg Highway and the Macedonia Road, now known as Highway 89. My family helped "Brother Eb" work on his family farm while my father worked at the Camden War Production Plant or the Pine Bluff Arsenal, doing support work as a carpenter. When Doyle came home on leave, he and his now-wife Margaret were married by Brother Eb in that house. Our family, along with Brother Eb, went to the Saline River to celebrate by camping and fishing. My family had a similar celebration when the war finally ended.

In the summer of 1945, my family moved from Brother Eb White's place to an old schoolhouse towards Warren. It was mostly one large room with a few small rooms that I can only assume were used for private offices and storage. We lived there until around November of that year. Over Thanksgiving, we moved about a hundred miles away to Jacksonville, Arkansas. I attended the rest of my fourth grade year in Jacksonville. Mother, Father, Bill, Mick, Nina, Victor, Cecil and I all lived at 393 Pike Avenue in a duplex. We had three small bedrooms — one for my parents, one for the girls, and one for the boys. I remember Bill preferred to sleep on the couch in the living room. This was our first home that had electricity, running water, and a bathroom. My mother especially loved this house. In the late summer of 1946, we moved from Jacksonville to Pleasant Valley again. We hated to leave the Jacksonville home with all its bells and whistles, but my grandmother had cancer and needed someone to care for her. My mother volunteered, so we moved to a permanent home.

Chapter 2

A Young Man's Adventures

I graduated from Warren High School in May of 1954, at the age of 17. I really wanted to go to college, but I did not have the information, the preparation, or the funds to do so. This caused me to turn to the military recruiters who came to our school.

The Army program had the most appeal to me. They would allow you to select a trade-type school that you wanted to attend — provided you passed the entrance exam — if you enlisted within 30 days. The Navy and the Air Force did not give you a choice; they selected the school they would put you into and required a four-year commitment. The Army was only three years, and I would be able to use GI benefits for college when I got out.

I decided to go to radar technician school and took the exam as soon as I graduated from high school. After I passed the test, the Army gave me a letter confirming that I could go to that school after I completed my basic training. So, on June 22, 1954, my dad took me to the bus station in Warren, gave me some fatherly advice — "Son, keep your priorities in order and you'll always be all right." — and then sent me off to join the Army.

I took the bus to Pine Bluff, about 50 miles away, where the recruiting office was. I went through the enlistment process there, and then got on another bus that evening to go to Little Rock's YMCA to spend the night with hundreds of other recruits from Arkansas.

The next morning, we all got up early and went into an auditorium in the YMCA. When we got there, we were told to line up around the walls of the gym. Then we were told to strip. Within a minute or two, there were about 100 of us recruits standing there naked.

There was a doctor sitting in a chair with a couple of medics standing on either side of him as a makeshift "doctor's office" for us to visit. We were told to just circle the gym very slowly and stop there by the doctor's "office." When you stopped, the two medics would stick you with a needle in each hip. After your shots, you were told to redress. After everyone had received their shots, a sergeant was put in charge of us. We then were sworn into our different services: the Army, the Navy, or the Air Force.

Our sergeant told us, "You're in the Army now." I will never forget the words that followed. He continued, "You're in the Army now. You are not here to think. We will tell you what to do. If you keep your ears open and your mouth shut and do exactly what you are told, you will do okay and be okay. And if you do not, you will wish you had, if you survive to make that wish. From now on, for the next eight weeks, for me or whoever is here in my place, I am your brain. And you'd better pay attention to your brain or you will wish you had."

I wasn't going to go against those instructions, I knew he meant what he said; not going against these instructions kept me out of trouble.

Those of us going into the Army got on a couple of big Greyhound buses and went to Fort Chaffee to begin our eight weeks of basic training. When we arrived, we were each given a uniform, which included boots and all. We had to put on the uniform and turn in our civilian clothes which were shipped back to our home addresses.

The next day, everybody went to a "barbershop" where they gave us what they called a GI haircut. All they did really was take some clippers and run them over your head, down to the skin, as close as they could get. When you came out of there, you had no hair at all on your head, except maybe a little bit of stubble like a five o'clock shadow on your head.

Then, we went into training. Every morning, we were up at five. We had a half hour of physical training at five thirty, breakfast at six, then military formation at seven. From then until dark, we trained all day, every day, doing various sorts of training. Some of it was classroom training, including some training in military history and tactics, as well as military law. Of course, we also did a lot of marching; you had to train to march.

At the time, the Korean conflict had not officially ended. We were training to fight in the conflict, and our trainers were all Korean War veterans. I had volunteered, hoping to eventually get to go to Korea when my training was complete. A cease-fire was in effect but neither side had surrendered at the time.

I was not assigned to go to Korea, but I saw a couple of major incidents while I was in training that brought home the realities of combat.

The first was when we were being trained to throw live hand grenades. First, they had us throw some dummy grenades, so we would know how to do it properly. You had to pull the pin out of the grenade, which loaded it, setting it to explode. It would explode 10 seconds after you pulled the pin out. The sergeant demonstrated the process. Then, each man would throw one live hand grenade.

What you had to do, as the sergeant demonstrated, was pull the pin out and count off seven seconds — then throw the grenade at a distance away from where the squad was standing. It would explode in three seconds and was designed to kill anybody in the near vicinity. If you were within 10 feet you were at least going to be badly injured, and within five feet you would most likely be killed.

Each one of us took our turn, including me, but one young soldier pulled the pin and then froze. He gripped the grenade with his hand and did not throw it. The sergeant saw immediately what he was doing and screamed at him to throw the grenade, but he did not. He just stood there.

The sergeant grabbed his arm, trying to rip the grenade from his hand and throw it forward, but it fell to the ground when he pulled it away from the young soldier. There was no time to pick it up and throw it safely. The sergeant threw himself on top of it and was killed immediately.

It was shocking to see. He had survived combat against the North Koreans, and in his preparation to train recruits, he had been told this sort of thing could happen. When this situation happened, the trainer was to protect the troops in whatever way possible, and he did. He gave his life to protect his troops, right there on the training field, saving at least three or four lives and preventing many others from injury. We never knew what happened to the recruit who froze. We never saw him again.

On another occasion, we were training to crawl under live machine gun fire. We were warned what would happen if we did not follow the strict orders we were given.

The machine guns were arranged along one side of a field and set up for automatic fire. One squad at a time would crawl across the field, 10 or 12 men all crawling parallel to each other.

You were to crawl on your elbows and knees and keep your head down, with the first run being without live fire. However, to complete that part of the training, you had to do it once with live fire 18 inches above the ground. You had to crawl on your belly, slide yourself along, and make sure you stayed down below the 18-inch level.

My group was waiting its turn while another group worked its way across the field. Suddenly, one kid screamed and jumped up and was killed on the spot. Apparently, he had come upon a rattlesnake — there were a lot of rattlesnakes around Chaffee — and he panicked.

It was a stark realization of what could happen in a war zone. And that war zone was what we were being trained for, to be able to do these kinds of things without panicking. We had had training in all sorts of firearms and other things. This training solidified the idea that you had to follow instructions and what would happen if you did not.

In all, we went through eight weeks of that type of training. The guys who goofed up by not following instructions, or by doing things they were not supposed to do, would be "washed back." This pushed troublemakers back two weeks to repeat that segment of training. If a recruit did this too many times, they would be put in a stockade.

Those who had volunteered mostly stayed out of trouble. The draftees, who did not want to be there in the first place, would do everything they could think of to try to get washed out of the Army. They did not care what their record said; they just did not want to be there. A company that started out with 200 men might be down to 160 by the time they finished training. Before a recruit could be washed out of the Army, they would spend extensive amounts of time in the stockade, similar to prisoners in "the hole."

I stayed out of trouble. I was only 17 at that time, but they made me an assistant squad leader. I only made that about two weeks before the training was up, but it was kind of an honor to be put there.

During basic training, we were all buck privates, classified as Enlisted 1 or E1. Our pay was $78 a month plus room and board. At the end of the training we had a graduation ceremony, with the general there to see us graduate. When we graduated, we got our first promotion to E2, a raise of $10, and a "uniform allowance" of $12 a month.

The end of basic training also meant a 10-day leave, which was the first real vacation I had ever had in my life. When I was growing up, we might go fishing for a weekend or something, but our family always worked whenever we could. So, having a 10-day paid vacation was just another reason why I liked the Army as much as I did.

That vacation meant that I could go home. I was given travel pay to get from Chaffee to my home, and from there to Fort Monmouth, New Jersey, for my training school. The Army would have given me a bus ticket if I wanted it, but if you took the pay you could buy a bus ticket and still have some money left over, so I elected to do that instead.

I spent most of my 10 days at home. It was a new experience, having a little money in my pocket, being able to do what I wanted to do, and not having to worry about working the next day. I saw a lot of my family and my school friends and then planned my travel to Fort Monmouth, New Jersey.

I chose the Greyhound bus because it was the cheapest way to get there. When I got off the bus in New York City, I went from the bus station to the famous Grand Central Station, where I got on a train to Fort Monmouth, which was considered the showplace of the Army. It was like a college campus, and I spent the next nine months going to school there.

I passed the test for admission to radar technology school, but within a day or two I realized I was in over my head. I was the youngest in a class of 15 to 20 men, most of whom had at least some college background while I had just graduated from high school. The course was highly technical with math and science at a level I had never studied. I tried hard for about three weeks but realized that I needed to get out of there. The math was just too far beyond me; I would wash out if I didn't do something and that would mean being sent to the infantry.

I asked the instructor for the morning off to go to the school administrator. I told the colonel who was in charge of the school that I knew I was in over my head and asked if I could transfer to another school. He looked at my records and said that I should not have been put into that school with only a high school education. He told me they did not normally allow transfers, but he would give me one chance.

We looked at the choices and decided on another nine-month school for telephone and radio teletype equipment repair. I took the test right there in his office and passed it, so he arranged for me to go to the other school, where I did just fine. There were 12 of us in the school and I finished second highest.

Along with school, there was also plenty of fun to be had during my time at Fort Monmouth. There were some wonderful beaches nearby. The Army base was right next to Asbury Park, New Jersey, and within a few miles were nice beaches at Red Branch and Long Branch. I dated a couple of local girls there. One was a student nurse that I met at church. She was a couple of years older than me and she had a car.

She invited me to go to New York to hear Billy Graham preach. Well, I had never heard of Billy Graham, but I was extremely interested, and he was at Madison Square Garden, where I had never been. We took her car and she told me to drive.

I could drive very well in Arkansas, but I had never driven in New York or New Jersey before. She was my navigator and got me into New York City and close to Madison Square Garden when I made a left turn and suddenly saw six sets of headlights coming toward me. I was going the wrong way on a one-way street! I managed to get turned around and we eventually found Madison Square Garden, where I heard Billy Graham preach for the first time.

During my training at Fort Monmouth, we went to school five days a week and were off on Saturday and Sunday. We usually drew kitchen police (KP) duty about once a month, which meant working in the kitchen for about 16 hours. Since I was always trying to save money for any weekend plans I might have, I would often work KP for somebody else who had the duty and they would pay me $10 for my 16 hours of work.

One of my classmates there was Bill Stanton, who became a lifelong friend. Bill was from Bristol, Pennsylvania, right near Philadelphia, which was not too far away. He liked to go home on weekends to visit his family and girlfriend and, as we became friends, I would go with him. We would hitchhike there on Friday evening, spend the weekend, then hitchhike back on Sunday.

At Christmas, I got a 10-day leave, so I went home to Arkansas to visit my friends and family. I returned to Fort Monmouth to complete my nine months of school and graduated in mid-June.

We had to fill out a form saying where we wanted to be assigned when we got out of school. I put Korea down as my request, but the fighting there had stopped, and they did not need any more of us there. There were 12 of us in the class, so we received a list of 12 positions. The guy who finished first in the class got first choice of the 12 positions, I finished second, so I got second choice, and so on. There was one position for

Alaska in the 12 they sent down — this was my choice. Why? I was always looking for a new experience. I had a 10-day leave to go home before going to Alaska where I got to take the first of many, many plane rides.

At the end of my leave I took a bus from Pine Bluff to Los Angeles, where I changed buses and headed to Fort Lewis, Washington.

I was to be processed out of Fort Lewis to go to Alaska. The processing took several days, and then I was scheduled to ship out on a big troop ship. I was excited about this prospect, as I had never been on a big ship and I wanted that experience. We then learned that some troops would be transported by plane. Well, I had already had my first plane flight and I really wanted to go by ship.

So the next morning during formation, they started calling out names of people to fall out and board a plane for Alaska. My name was called, but I figured as no one there knew me, so I just stood there and let them pass me by. They filled my slot on the plane with someone else and the formation was dismissed. I went to sick call pretending to have some ailment, then reported back to my unit after the plane had left.

My little ploy worked. That afternoon I was processed to get on the ship. The next day I boarded the ship, with about a thousand other troops, and we shipped out from the Port of Seattle headed to Alaska. It was a beautiful five-day trip with one night being docked at Kodiak Island, the largest island on the Aleutian chain. We docked in Alaska at the Port of Whittier, the southern point of the Alaskan railroad. We then transferred from the ship to a troop train to travel to Ladd Air Force Base near Fairbanks, Alaska.

The train covered about 600 miles of beautiful scenery. It traveled through Anchorage, past Mt. McKinley in McKinley National Park, to the northern end of the railroad in Fairbanks,

Alaska. From Fairbanks, we were bused out to Ladd Air Force Base. I was assigned to Headquarters Company, Yukon Command, which was located on the base. I checked in there and learned that I would be working out of Eielson Air Force Base, 26 miles south of Fairbanks.

I arrived in Alaska in mid-July 1955. Little did I know that I would spend most of the next 13 years there. I went into the shop at Eielson as a radio teletypewriter repairman. After I had been at Eielson eight or nine months, the Army moved our shop to Ladd Air Force Base. At about that time, my supervisor — the "Wire Chief" — was an E7 and I was an E4 by then.

My supervisor left and I was moved up to his job, but all the ranks had been frozen because so many were coming out of the Korean War so I never got the extra stripes and pay that went with the position. So I served in the E7 slot with the rank of E4 for the rest of the time I was in the Army.

One experience while I was at the Air Force base sticks out in my mind more than anything else. I had walked roughly two blocks from my barracks to the base's photo laboratory where I had developed and printed some photos. For context, the Eielson Air Force Base had an exceedingly long runway for many F-84 fighter jets and B-52 bombers. The barracks for the headquarters was right next to this runway.

It was freezing cold, about 30 degrees below zero. While returning to my barracks, I saw some F-84 fighter jets and B-52 bombers taking off. One of the fighter jets began to roll onto its right side at roughly 200 feet off the ground, where it then turned and passed in front of me! It skimmed roughly 50–75 feet above the ground. I watched the pilot who, luckily, was the only person in the plane, struggle with controlling the plane. The plane stayed airborne for a quarter of a mile, then hit the second story of a military department residence, going through the first building and hitting two other buildings before exploding. Unfortunately, 14 people were killed alongside the pilot. One of those killed was my first sergeant; he had gone home to have lunch with his family. When the crash occurred, I ran to see if I could be of any help. Knowing there was nothing I could do and having my camera with me, I took some photos of the wreckage to document what had happened.

Before I left Eielson for Ladd, my company commander called me in. He was a captain and a West Point graduate. He asked me about my future, and I told him I was looking forward to getting out of the Army and using my GI Bill benefits to go to college. He had reviewed my records and offered to give me a recommendation to go to West Point. We talked about it, and I informed him that I did not really want to commit to another four years on the East Coast at West Point.

Then he told me about Officer Candidate School (OCS). I could take a test for it, and if I passed it would be six months of school, after which I would be a second lieutenant. It seemed worth considering, so I took the test — both the physical and a large battery of officer tests — and I was approved for the program. The catch was that you had to be 21 when you graduated from the candidate school, and I would still be 20 when I finished my three-year enlistment, so I would have to re-enlist for another three years. I was unsure about the prospect of another three years, especially with ranks being frozen, so I put off making that decision.

If I did not re-enlist, I would be due to get out of the Army in June of 1957. As that time approached, I had the standard re-enlistment talk with the executive officer of my company. He asked about my plans and I told him I was all set up for OCS. He advised me to take my release and get my degree in a civilian college instead, as I had originally planned. Then if I still wanted to be in the Army, I could come back through the college programs, which would offer a better career path.

I was still only 20 years old and I looked up to him, so I took his advice. I did not actually get a discharge since my period of enlistment was three years active duty and five years reserves. I got a release at the end of my three years of active duty. For the next five years I remained in the reserves, which meant I could be called up anytime on 24-hour notice, but I was never called up.

I took my release right there at Ladd Air Force Base. Just as on my past leaves, they gave me travel pay to get home. They would give you so much per mile, and it was always more than you would spend if you traveled economically. You could leave yourself a little extra money if you just took the cash and made your own travel arrangements.

I applied for school at the University of Arkansas and was accepted to enter that fall. My plan was to look for a job and earn a little extra money in Alaska before heading home, since you could make more money there than in Arkansas.

The employment office in Fairbanks sent me out to a job that proved to be quite an opportunity. The well-known author Edna Ferber had been staying in Fairbanks writing what would become her novel *Ice Palace*. Having finished the book, she was planning to leave Alaska and was looking for some temporary help packing up.

I went to her apartment, we talked a little, and she hired me. She said she would need me for about a week. I went to work for her every day, helping her pack up. She had a brand new 1957 Plymouth Belvedere and was planning to drive back to the East Coast. A day or two before we finished, she made me an offer and I have regretted ever since that I turned it down.

She said that she was driving her car back to the East Coast and asked if I would be interested in going with her to help with the driving. We would stop at motels or roadhouses at night, and when we got to New York, I could stay for a few days or just head back. She would pay me a generous amount and buy me a plane ticket to Arkansas and back to Fairbanks. I thought about it a bit but said no since I had planned to stay in Fairbanks the rest of the summer. I did not realize at the time how esteemed and well-known she was; if I had, I might have answered differently. It would have been a wonderful experience.

There was not much time for regret, though, because the employment office had another job offer waiting for me. It was a good opportunity, a high-paying summer job in the communication station up on Barter Island. It was one of several radar stations operated by the federal government to monitor all the air traffic. Even though there were military people there, they hired civilians to work in the communication station. At the time, the United States government was concerned with Russian airplanes violating U.S. air space due to the Cold War. Since I had the training, experience, and all the clearances from my military service, they wanted me to go up there and do exactly what I had been doing at the base. I worked there the rest of the summer. The pay was particularly good, and it was an interesting job. At the end of the summer, they made me an almost irresistible offer — an 18-month contract with two 30-day paid leaves, and round trip plane tickets to Arkansas — but I turned them down because I wanted to get into college.

I flew back to Fairbanks around the first of September. My oldest sister, Grachel, was living about 100 miles south of Fairbanks, where her husband, a career military man, was stationed at the time. So I rented a car and drove down to visit them. When I got back to Fairbanks, I bought my ticket to leave at midnight. I had a dinner date that night with a girl I had been dating. She was going to take me to the airport and turn in the rental car.

With about four hours to kill before I was to pick my date up, I went out to the University of Alaska campus just outside of Fairbanks. I went into the controller's office just to pick up a catalog to browse through on my way home that night. The controller was a fellow named Harold Bird. He saw me and must have realized I was not a regular student there, so he started talking with me and led me back into his office. Without me even realizing his sales pitch, he had me sold on at least one semester of the University of Alaska before returning home to the University of Arkansas. That same afternoon of our conversation, I registered for classes using my GI Bill benefits, and got a room. They had a special dorm for veterans that came with special privileges. I then went to the airport and cashed in my ticket. With a little money in my pocket, I picked up my date, took her to dinner and told her I was not leaving Alaska just yet.

Little did I know how that impulsive decision would change the course of my whole life.

I started college that same week, registered as a pre-law student majoring in history and political science. My first class in the morning was an English refresher course, and when I walked in on the first day of class, I looked around and saw an open seat next to a cute little blonde, curly-haired girl with an infectious smile. I sat next to her — Kay Kelly — and that was the day that changed my life.

That first class was an orientation, but the professor did give us an assignment. We were each asked to write a personal essay, talking about our background, our philosophy of life, and our desires for the future, and the essay would be graded.

It so happened that both of us had the next hour after class free, so I asked that little blonde, curly-haired girl if she would like to go to the snack shop with me. I bought coffee, but I was taken aback when she told me she wanted pickles and ice cream. But there was no cause for alarm. It turned out that she was a diabetic and she needed some ice cream for her blood sugar.

Over our snacks we got better acquainted. I learned that Kay was only 17; she had come to college straight out of high school. She had grown up in Fairbanks and lived only a few miles from the university.

When we got our graded essays back, Kay asked if she could read mine. So we read each other's papers, which told me a little bit more about her and her a little bit more about me, and I liked what I read. Her essay was thoughtful and serious, and I realized that we shared a philosophy.

We started dating and it was not long before our relationship warmed up. I met her family — her mother Catherine, her dad Beryl, and her older brother and sister. Kay's parents had been in Alaska since about 1930. Beryl had worked in the gold mines and the coal mines, then worked for the military during World War II. After the war he bought some property and went into business for himself where he became a successful businessman with a Jeep auto dealership and a Firestone tire distributorship.

Kay and I dated through the school year. We hit a little bump over the Christmas holidays. We were out of school for about two weeks, but I was working part-time as a security guard at the local hospital to earn a little extra money. During the break from classes I worked extra hours, 12 hours every day. Kay was driving my car, taking me to work and picking me up afterward so she could use my car while I was working. However, I realized that I needed to spend more time with Kay to help our relationship flourish, so I quit working so much.

Semester break came in mid-January, and we decided to take a road trip with another couple, Georgia Clark and Bob

Summers. The four of us headed to Anchorage, about 400 miles away, in Kay's Jeepster. We spent three or four days there.

On the way to Anchorage, we stopped at the home of my sister Grachel and her husband Hudie. Grachel cooked up a big meal for the four of us and we had a good time there. Grachel was the first member of my family that Kay met, and the only one she met before we were married.

It was a good trip and it gave us a good opportunity to get to know each other better. We returned to Fairbanks and went back to school. But within a few months I needed to make plans for the summer and fall, and I had some important decisions to make.

My affection for Kay had grown to love, and Kay expressed the same for me. I had planned to return to Arkansas at the end of the school year in May, and then enter the University of Arkansas in the fall, but I was not sure how Kay would feel about that.

We had not really discussed marriage, but I realized I did not want to make plans without her, so I decided to ask her to marry me. If she said yes, we could start planning our life together. If she said no, I would finish the school year and then go back to Arkansas. I really was not sure what she would say.

So, in mid-February I bought an engagement ring and took Kay out to dinner. When I took her back to her dorm, I parked at the curb, showed her the ring, and proposed to her right there sitting in the car. She said yes.

We talked a bit about the future, and I told her to pick the date for our wedding. She chose Nov. 1, 1958, which would be her 19th birthday. That would give us a nine-month engagement. We decided we would take a year off from school and travel to Arkansas after the wedding.

I got a summer job working for the National Park Service at what was then called Mount McKinley National Park. As soon as school finished in late May, I said goodbye to Kay for the summer — or so I thought — and took the train down to the park.

A couple of weeks after I started working, Kay arrived at the park to visit for a couple of days. I got her set up in the park hotel, and while she was there, she talked to the hotel manager and got herself a job for the summer as a maid. So we took the train back to Fairbanks, packed up Kay's Jeepster, and drove it back to the park. We spent a delightful summer there, enjoying the scenery, the wildlife, and each other's company on our days off. We stayed there until the park closed its visitor facilities in September, then returned to Fairbanks.

Kay moved back in with her parents until the wedding, and I accepted a job working for her father. My sister Grachel's husband was being transferred out of Alaska, so they offered to sell me their mobile home. I arranged to move the trailer to a lot that I had purchased on the edge of Fairbanks, and that was where I lived until the wedding.

Our wedding was planned for Nov. 1, which was Kay's 19th birthday and three days after my 22nd birthday.

Kay and her mother planned the wedding. It was overwhelming to me, as all I could think of was the movie *Father of the Bride*. Kay's dad was very calm, cool, and collected, but I was just an observer. I knew nothing about big weddings. Where I came from, weddings happened with a preacher at your home, or maybe go to church and have the two congregations with their own friends. This was different. This was *the* town event.

We were married in the Fairbanks Evangelical Lutheran Church and had our reception in the basement of the church, with about 300 guests. There was no one from my family there as my family just did not have the money to travel all the way to Alaska, and nobody really expected them to anyway. And the Kellys were very gracious. Kay's brother Bud served as my best man, and Kay's best friend Judy was her maid of honor. After the wedding and reception, Bud and Judy drove us to the Traveler's Inn, which was the fanciest hotel in Fairbanks at the time, where we spent the night.

The next morning, we went over to Kay's parents' home. We loaded up her Jeepster with our belongings and emergency supplies, then set out for the Alcan Highway on a 2,500 mile road trip down to the lower 48 — our first trip as a married couple. I was no longer alone.

Chapter 3

Married Life

OUR VERY FIRST ADVENTURE as a married couple was the 2,500-mile trip over the Alcan and Alaskan Highway. I had never driven it before, as I had arrived in Alaska by ship, and traveled back and forth to Arkansas by plane, so this trip was a fresh experience to me. Not to mention, since it was November, we would be traveling in wintertime conditions, adding a whole new layer to the complexity of our excursion. My new father-in-law, Beryl, who had driven the highway many times, made sure to give me a thorough orientation before we left. We were to expect heavy snow, high mountains, and below-zero temperatures.

That first day, we drove about 200 miles before stopping at a place called Fortymile Roadhouse. The owners of the roadhouse were friends of the Kellys, so Kay had acquaintances there and we spent the night. We left the next morning to continue our trip to Seattle, the first leg of our journey.

It took us about a week to reach Seattle. I was an experienced driver, but this was something new for me. It was bitter cold — 40 below in some places — and there was *lots* of snow. The road was not only frozen and isolated, but also crooked and mountainous until we were about 400 miles out of Seattle.

However, despite all of the frozen bumps in the road, it was a good trip.

Our destination in Seattle was the home of Kay's sister, Dorothy Vring, who lived in Ballard, Seattle with her husband, Jim, and their daughters.

Our stop in Seattle was not just to visit family. Kay's father had arranged for her to have some extensive dental work there, so we expected to stay in Seattle for about a month. We stayed with Dorothy's family for a week, then moved into a little efficiency apartment in a motel. I took a job as a riveter at Boeing Aircraft, figuring I would work while Kay had her dental work done.

To get to Boeing in time for my early shift, I had to leave our little apartment about five in the morning. While I got ready for work, Kay would get up, fix breakfast, and make me a lunch. One morning, during my second or third week at Boeing, I was in the shower when I heard a loud bang outside the bathroom door.

I opened the bathroom door to find Kay lying in the floor, unconscious and in a convulsion. It seemed she had fallen and had probably hit her head. It was insulin shock, the result of extremely low blood sugar. I had seen her have insulin reactions before, and before we got married, her mother had arranged for me to talk with Kay's doctor about her diabetes, but this was more than I ever expected. We did not have a phone in that apartment, and since this was long before cell phones, I yanked on some pants, ran to the apartment manager, asked him to call an ambulance. As he was doing that, I rushed back to Kay. She was still unconscious, with her eyes rolled back in her head. I made sure she had not swallowed her tongue.

By the time the ambulance arrived I had wrapped Kay's robe around her and gotten dressed myself. When we got in the ambulance, I told them to take us to Virginia Mason

Hospital in Seattle, about eight miles away. I knew that they would have medical records because Kay's parents had sent her there for treatment previously, so off we went, lights flashing and siren blaring.

At Virginia Mason, they stabilized her by getting her on a glucose drip, then started doing blood tests and so forth. While they were taking care of her, I went to call her sister's home and realized that when I had put on my clothes, I did not even think of my wallet or change. I did not have a penny on me.

One of the nurses called Kay's sister's home, and my brother-in-law, Jim, came to the hospital. Kay was unconscious for a few hours. When she woke up a few hours later, Jim was out of the room. Kay's eyes opened and she just looked at me and said, "Well, where am I?"

I said, "It's okay; we're in Seattle. You've been in insulin shock."

And she said, "Seattle? What am I doing in Seattle?"

It quickly became clear that Kay had no recent memory. She could not remember anything for the last three or four months, which meant she did not remember driving to Seattle over the highway. She did not even remember our getting married.

She knew me, and knew that we were engaged, but everything for the past several months was a blank. It was not until she saw Jim that she finally believed that we were really in Seattle. Over the course of the day, things started to come back to her gradually — not all at once — and by the end of the day her memory had returned up until the last few hours.

Once she got her memory back and seemed stable, the hospital released her and I took her back to our apartment. Kay recovered quickly and was back to normal in about 24 hours, but I did call in and take off work for a few days.

This was my first of many such experiences of Kay having severe insulin reactions. It was a challenge in the early years of our marriage; it took many years before her diabetes came under better control.

About a week after this episode, Kay's mother flew down from Alaska. I suspect that Jim and Dorothy told her what had happened, and she was concerned about Kay. So, she spent a couple of days with them and then came to stay with us for an extended visit. By then, we had moved into a small efficiency apartment in an apartment complex. Kay's mother stayed with us for a couple of weeks. I think it was mainly just to make sure Kay was okay because she knew I was inexperienced with diabetes even though she had tried to educate me about it.

Our apartment was tiny, just one room and a kitchenette. The bed was a couch that folded down from the wall. We got a cot for her mom to sleep on, but the only place to put it was beside our bed. We spent two weeks — in just the second month of our marriage — sleeping next to my mother-in-law, putting a small strain on us as newlyweds.

We stayed longer in Seattle than we had planned due to Kay's dental work. I left my job at Boeing because I did not want to leave Kay alone so much, and I got a job working at a garage. Over those few months, we made friends and visited family, as Kay had extended family in Washington. However, by April, we were ready to move on to Arkansas as we had originally planned. When we left Seattle at the end of April, we first drove over to Walla Walla, in central Washington, to visit with Kay's Grandma Kelly, who was elderly and had cancer.

After spending a couple of nights there, we headed on toward Arkansas. We drove the 2,300 miles from Walla Walla to Mother and Dad's home in Warren, Arkansas in less than five days. We stopped in Pocatello, Idaho for an overnight visit with a friend of Kay's, had dinner with an old Army buddy of mine in Denver, and then drove straight through to Arkansas. We got into Arkansas that Friday afternoon.

We called ahead to let my family know we were coming, so they had planned a big dinner at my brother Doyle's house. There were probably 50 or 60 people and they had a big welcome party. It was Kay's first introduction to the Myers family, except for my sister Grachel, who had been in Alaska when we were there. It was a bit overwhelming for Kay, who was used to a small family. She was inundated with new relatives, but everyone loved her right away and she responded in kind.

We had expected to settle there in Arkansas, and I planned to go back to college. But life had other plans for us.

Within a few weeks, as the summer began, Kay developed allergies so severe that they even affected her diabetes. Finally, the doctor told her that she really needed a different climate.

Since it was clear we would have to move, we figured that we might as well go back to Alaska, where we had roots. We contacted Kay's parents and told them that we were going to have to leave Arkansas. Her dad encouraged us to come back to Alaska and sent us a little money to help make the move. So, we left our car, which I had bought in Seattle, with my parents and my dad took over the payments. Then we took a train to Seattle and flew from there back to Fairbanks.

Kay's dad offered me a good job working for him as a salesman, and we moved into a mobile home behind the business. In September, I went back to the University of Alaska, where I would take early morning classes and then work the rest of the day. In the meantime, Kay did some babysitting; she loved being around children and was eager for us to begin our own family — before we were married, she told me she would like to have a dozen children!

Kay had gotten pregnant just a couple of months after we married, but she miscarried so early in the pregnancy that she did not even know when it happened. The doctor told her that she had miscarried and advised her not to get pregnant again right away because of her youth and her diabetes. She was heartbroken.

We had been back in Alaska for a few months when we were approached by a social worker, Coleen Redman, who was also a Kelly family friend. Coleen oversaw a foster care program in Fairbanks and asked if we might be interested in keeping foster children. Of course, we said yes immediately and Coleen initiated the licensing process. At that time, Kay was 20 years old and I was 23. We filled out all the applications and went through the official background investigation to get approved as foster parents. We moved out of the mobile home and rented a better, bigger apartment.

In March of 1960, we got a call from my brother-in-law Hurley telling us that my dad had died of a heart attack. Kay and I made the trip back to Arkansas for the funeral and stayed there about a week visiting family and friends. My mother, who did not drive, gave me back the car I had originally given to my father the year before. We drove the approximately 5,000 miles from Arkansas to Fairbanks. But by the time we returned to Fairbanks in early April, I had missed too many class sessions to make up, so I withdrew from the university and started considering other types of work.

I applied to the Fairbanks Police Department and in June was hired as a police officer. I would spend about two years with the department, and for the most part, it was a good experience.

After training, my first two months were spent working in the jail. Then I was moved to foot patrol, and spent about three months patrolling the downtown streets and bars. At that time, Fairbanks was a pretty rugged wild town, with a lot of drinking and scandalous behavior. When I started doing foot patrol, my training officer was a sergeant who had been there a while. He told me that there were 32 bars and 32 churches in Fairbanks, which was a city of about 13,000 people. It was a frontier life.

In one of Fairbanks' many bars, my trainer introduced me to an Indian woman named Nevada. The town was full of what were called the night girls — the prostitutes — and at one point Nevada got into an argument with one of the prostitutes over their mutual boyfriend, a cab driver. And instead of working it out in some way, they just decided to have a duel.

Both women were packing pistols. So they walked outside the bar, turned back to back, paced off 10 steps, then turned and started shooting. Nevada shot and killed the other woman. She was arrested, but she pleaded self-defense, and they made a deal. She served one year in jail for killing the other woman in the duel. This story tells you what Fairbanks was like in 1960.

After about three months on foot patrol, I went on motor patrol. Whenever I could, I volunteered for investigative assignments, and I found I loved that work.

When I had 15 months on the force, an opening came up for promotion to sergeant. The requirement for promotion was one year on the force plus passing written and oral exams. When an opening came up, there was no need to apply; everyone who was eligible had a chance to take the tests. Only eight people qualified for the promotion and even though I was the youngest in age and the newest in time of service, I got the promotion. Suddenly, I was the supervisor of some guys senior to me and that did not go over very well, leading to some resentment from the older officers.

I stayed there another year. I learned a lot not only about the department but also about the court system. In many ways, I enjoyed the work and it was a good experience, but as I gained some seniority, I also began to see problems that left me disillusioned. I saw people being protected or prosecuted according to the discretion and decisions of officers and prosecutors and not necessarily according to the law. I saw injustices happening at the hands of some of my fellow officers, and I had no way to change that.

There was one incident that was the last straw for me. I was working with a police captain one night when we got word of a house fire. We went to the site around midnight. Once the firefighters had finished and pulled away, we talked to the woman who had been living alone in the house.

Apparently, the captain knew her from some past connection. He asked her why she decided to burn her house. I still remember her response.

She called him by name and said: "I didn't burn the house. I didn't have anything to do with it."

And he hit her. He just drew back and hit her face. He hit her so hard that she went all the way across the room, hitting the wall on the other side. I had a hard time believing what I was seeing, but I knew that if I made a complaint against him, it would never fly. She might have had a criminal record, but nothing connected with this house.

I stewed about that for a couple of days and I decided I could not continue. I wrote a letter of resignation and took it in to the chief, who asked me what had happened. I did not give him the details; I only told him that I could not continue to work in that atmosphere. He asked me to stay, but I resigned anyway. I did not even have another job lined up. The chief wrote me a nice letter of recommendation and told me that I could come back if I ever wanted to do that.

I left the police department behind and moved on. I spent the next six months selling cars. It was not something that I wanted to do for life, but it was an easy job and it paid better than police work.

While I was on the police department, I began to train as a pilot. A good friend and fellow police officer had a license and

I flew with him. I took lessons and after six hours of training, I soloed. After that I could rent a plane and fly by myself. After 40 hours of flying, I took my test and could take passengers. I also took training in instrument flying for safety's sake. I trained in several planes, including the Cessna 150, 172, and 180; the Piper Cherokee 140; and the Taylorcraft Tail-Dragger. I enjoyed flying and used those skills in both Alaska and Arkansas for a number of years.

During all these changes in my professional life, there had been big changes on the home front as well.

I would begin to take on a new title: Dad. Around the time that I was accepted to the police department, in June 1960, Kay and I received word that we had been approved for a foster care license. We could take up to three children, and we eagerly awaited our first foster child.

We did not wait long. Within a very short time, Coleen Redman brought us our first foster child. She was almost three years old, a full-blooded Eskimo named Eleanore. We took her as our first foster child, and she stole our hearts right away. We adopted her about three years later and she became the first of our five children.

Although our foster child license was for up to three children, they started bringing us children almost immediately and we almost always had at least four children in our home. Every time I pointed out that we were only licensed for three, they would say, "Well, would you keep him or her until we make other arrangements?" Often, though, the other arrangements never got made.

One foster child, Esther, was with us for about five years. She came to us when she was 13 and stayed with us until she was 18, when she graduated from high school and went on to nursing school. Another of our girls was a teenager who had run away from Tennessee all the way to Alaska. I first met her in the juvenile detention. She was a challenge and she gave us a tough time for a while, but then she started seeing a neighborhood boy from down the street and they fell in love. We promised her that if she behaved herself, we would work things out. She stayed with us until she turned 18 and we gave her a church wedding. She wore Kay's wedding gown and I even gave her away.

Over a period of almost nine years, until we left Alaska for good, we fostered a total of 37 children. Some of the children were with us for only a short time, others for longer. However, caring for our growing family meant that I needed to seriously consider what my next professional career move would be. I did not want to continue to sell cars — rather, I wanted to put my background and skills to work.

One of the things I liked best about my time on the police force was investigative work. With the encouragement and advice of a local attorney, I decided to go into the private investigation business.

Another attorney, Bob Parish, was not only a family friend and a neighbor, but also a well-known and respected civil attorney. We had become acquainted while I was in the police department.

Bob needed an investigator, but he wanted to see an example of my work. He offered to give me one case as a test, and that became my first private investigation. In January 1963, we agreed that I would do the first case for four dollars an hour plus expenses, and eight cents per mile on my car. If Bob liked my work, he would then hire me as an investigator at eight dollars per hour.

That first case was a railroad intersection accident. A train had collided with a car at a crossing in Clear, Alaska, about 60 miles away. I drove down there and did what I thought would be an appropriate investigation, and while Bob was satisfied with my work, he wanted to show me a few things. So he started grading my work like a high school teacher would grade a student's paper. He told me he thought I could do this work and if I wanted to go ahead with it, he would hire me and teach me the things that I did not know.

I got both a job and an incredibly good teacher. Bob Parish remained a client of mine through his entire time practicing law. Although he was 20 years older than me, we became good friends.

We arranged that I would pursue other investigative work, but I would not take any work that conflicted with Bob's cases. I worked hard on building up a private investigation business in Fairbanks, and right from the beginning, Kay worked with me to build up the business, even as our family was growing and we were still raising foster children. We were a team in everything. I worked out of our house two or three months before moving into a small office in the Bank Building where I hired a secretary to assist me there.

One of my first cases was a referral from my former boss, the chief of police, Stan Zaveral. He referred me to a Mr. Thompson, a neighbor of his. Thompson was a bit of a mystery. Though he apparently had no regular job, he was obviously quite well off. He was suspected of being involved in criminal activities but had no record of being charged.

This referral became my first missing person case as Mr. Thompson, who was probably in his 50s, had a much younger girlfriend who had been living with him. The two had a big disagreement and afterward she disappeared. He wanted me to find her and get her to come back. I was supposed to tell her all would be forgiven if she would just come back to him.

I enlisted another ex-police officer, a former colleague, to assist me and the two of us located the girlfriend within 24 hours. She was in Anchorage, 400 miles away. She told me she was afraid to go back to him, but she had nowhere else to go. She was afraid he would have her killed. She asked for 24 hours to think it over.

I called Thompson and told him that I knew where she was, but I would not give him her location because she wanted 24 hours to consider her situation. He agreed but insisted that I not let her out of my sight. The next day at noon, she agreed to go back to talk with him. I think she had called him on the phone somewhere and talked with him, so we just put her in the car and drove her to his house and left her there. It was a strange case, but Thompson paid me very well, and from then on, he gave me other work until his death in a car accident a couple of years later.

The business was growing, and we started getting cases from several other attorneys in Fairbanks. Kay was a big help in building the business because her family was so well known there, and she would go to see prospective clients. I also expanded the business by adding security service as well as courier and process service.

It was during this time that I learned that one of my employees was pregnant and planning to give the baby up. Kay and I talked it over and we offered to adopt the baby, and that was how Lee came into our lives. We were at the hospital when he was born in April, 1964. This was not long after we adopted Ellen, so now we had two children of our own. At the same time, I was taking classes at the University of Alaska while we were working as hard as we could to build the business. The pace took its toll and we began to get burned out.

We made a long-term plan to leave Alaska eventually and try again to live in Arkansas. About that time, I was recruited by an acquaintance who had moved from Alaska to Oregon and was working with New York Life. He recruited me to work as an insurance salesman in the Portland, Oregon area. If I took this position, it meant that I had to sell my businesses.

The assistant chief of police, a man named John Arkels, heard about my plans, and offered to buy my business. We agreed to sell and made the decision to go to Portland.

So in March 1965, we left Fairbanks for Portland. We rented a house in a little town called Molalla, Oregon and I went to work for New York Life Insurance Company.

We spent a year in Molalla. While we loved it there, the insurance business did not suit me well and we began to struggle financially. I could not leave the investigation field behind completely; once in a while I would get a call from Bob Parish and I would fly back to Fairbanks to help him with a case.

One of those calls from Bob was a large injury case in February 1966. The plaintiff was a college classmate of mine who was now in law school. I helped Bob prepare the witnesses and stayed through the trial. When the trial was over and Bob had won a significant judgment for the young plaintiff, he asked me to consider coming back to Alaska. He said he would make it worth my while. I knew it would have to be an exceptionally good offer, as Kay really liked living in Molalla and I would have to persuade her to make the move. I told him I would need a guarantee of $1200 a month plus expenses for 30 hours a week of work, a flexible schedule so I could go back to college, and the option to accept work from other clients if they did not conflict with any of Bob's cases. I thought I had set the bar so high that he would not be able to afford it, but he surprised me.

Bob not only accepted my terms; he also wrote me a generous check right away. I flew back to Portland that night and talked to Kay about it. She understood, knowing that we were struggling financially down there, and Bob would be very generous to us. However, Kay had her own terms for moving back to Alaska. Since we had good connections there from our time as foster parents, she made me promise that we could adopt a third child when we got there. I promised that we would try. She also wanted a promise that we would not stay in Alaska more than a couple of years — even though she had grown up in Alaska, she was ready for a permanent move to the south.

I went back to Fairbanks and went to work for Bob. I bought a duplex house, with room for our family on one side and a renter on the other side and started fixing it up. Kay stayed in Molalla with the children until school was out that May.

In June, Kay arrived with our two children — Ellen was in kindergarten and Lee was two — and my 17-year-old nephew, Mike Myers, who was living with us while he finished high school. Kay immediately went to work on getting a third child, while I kept working with Bob and taking classes at the university.

We also started establishing another business of our own, the Telco Answering Service. I had been a client of theirs and when they were looking to sell, they asked me if I would consider buying the business. I bought it with Bob Parish's help, and Kay went to work as the manager. At the same time, we were taking in foster children again, along with our own two children and seeking a third child. Kay's efforts on that mission bore fruit quickly, and by late summer we were notified that we would have our third baby in January of 1967. Katy was born in the same hospital as Lee, and we took her home when she was three days old.

Chapter 4

The Great Flood

BY THE SPRING of '67 Kay and I were very busy but very happy with our family and our business. My work with Bob Parish continued to be a great learning experience as I always loved to learn, and it was a great opportunity to do so.

I was his firm's investigator, which meant that I investigated every new case his office accepted — mostly personal injury and product liability cases. Bob taught me how to prepare interrogatories and do other discovery work; when he went to trial, I did background investigations on jury members and helped prepare witnesses to testify.

The answering service was thriving — it was the only answering service in town — and we also served as a radio dispatcher for businesses that used radios, such as construction companies and the civil defense.

Then our busy routine was turned upside down when the Great Flood of 1967 hit Fairbanks. It was one of the worst disasters in Alaska's history.

Fairbanks is located in the Tanana Valley, with mountains on three sides. The Chena River, a tributary of the Tanana River, runs right through Fairbanks. The Chena is a good-sized river; paddle wheelers cruise up and down it. The river had no history of flooding as far as I know, but there had been a lot of snow in the mountains that winter. There was heavy rain in July, and then in August, the area got the heaviest rainfall in its history. With the combination of the snowmelt and the heavy rain, the Chena River started to rise quickly.

On August 14, Kay was at home and I was downtown working. About five o'clock in the afternoon, I left the office to go home and when I drove over the Chena River bridge, just a couple of blocks away, I saw how much the water had risen. The water level was normally 10 or 12 feet below the bridge, but it was now getting right up under the bridge. It was still raining heavily and I knew that was dangerous. I went home to check on Kay and the children. Mike had graduated high school and returned to Arkansas, and we had stopped taking in foster children, so it was just the two of us and our own three children.

When I called the answering service, our operator on duty told me the civil defense was using our emergency radios and was already evacuating people from low-lying areas. I thought our home would be safe, as it was about a mile from the river, so I told Kay I was going back downtown to help out with the emergency.

By the time I got back downtown, the water was coming over the bridge and was about four inches deep on Second Avenue, where our office was located. We were on the second floor of a building called The Co-Op Drugstore. When I went inside, water was already three or four inches deep on the floor of the drugstore and employees were busy trying to move merchandise to higher shelves. I went upstairs to our office where I stayed for almost the entirety of eight days.

The water rose to about six feet in the street outside, and four to five feet downstairs on the ground floor of the drugstore. Fortunately for those of us stuck there in the building, we had been careful to pick up food items from the snack bar, so at least we had some provisions. There were about 10 of us: people from other small offices in the building, one Telco employee and me. By morning, we could look down from the mezzanine to see that the water had reached the top of the display shelves downstairs. We could not go down there without getting into at least chest-high water.

The phones were out, so I could not reach Kay and the kids. Our radios were in the hands of the rescue workers, police, fire, and civil defense as we were dispatching for all of them. In the morning, I asked some fellows in one of the rescue boats to go by our house to check on Kay and the children. They radioed back that there was nobody in the house, but the car was under water. They said that everyone in that area had been evacuated to the University of Alaska campus, which was not far from our house.

The main university campus is on a hill probably 150 feet above the street level. Thousands of people had congregated up there. I figured Kay and the kids were among them, but I had no way to know for sure.

It was two days before I was able to get word of my family. I had everyone looking for them. Finally, one of the doctors helping evacuees at the university was able to connect us. He knew Kay and the kids, and he had one of our radios. He handed the radio to Kay and told her to talk to me so that I knew she was okay. She told me rescue workers had knocked on our door in the middle of the night, put her and the kids in a boat, and took them to the university. After several days, Kay's brother, Bud and his wife Lillian — who lived on higher ground — found that they could get to the campus via a back road, so they went out there and brought Kay and the children back to their house.

I stayed at the office dispatching rescue boats, helicopters, police, and fire fighters during the search-and-rescue effort. By my fifth day stranded at the office, I asked one of the helicopter crews if they would have time to pick me up from the roof of the Co-Op Building and take me out to where my wife and children were. They took me out to Bud's house and dropped me off, then came back two hours later to pick me up. I was able to see my family, get a shower, and eat a meal before heading back downtown. When I was picked up, the helicopter landed on the roof of the Co-Op Building and I went back to the office for another two days to dispatch radios until the water had receded enough so that everything was being done on land. We lost three cars in the flood.

Our answering service was shut down because the phone lines were down, but because our business was an emergency service, the utility company worked with us and we were back in operation three days after the water receded.

I borrowed a Volkswagen van from a friend and loaded two of our switchboards into the back. I parked the van next to the telephone company building and they ran a cable out their window and into the back of the van to give us immediate phone service. We operated out of that van for several weeks until the phone lines were repaired, and we could move back into our office.

The flood turned life upside down for the whole city of Fairbanks. Several people lost their lives, and the damage to businesses and homes was estimated at more than $200 million.

Fortunately, we were able to secure some disaster assistance funds to help with the business. On a personal level, most of our household furnishings were okay, although all three of our cars were ruined.

After the flood, we just went back to work. We continued to build the phone service and I again built a small private investigation and process service business that we ran out of the answering service office. I was still doing investigative work for Bob Parish and taking classes at the university.

Despite all this, Kay and I had not given up on our long-term plan to leave Alaska. We were tired of the long cold winters and wanted to raise our family in a warmer climate. Kay had been on medication to help with the allergies that had plagued her the last time we had tried to live in Arkansas, and we wanted to move closer to my family and to Kay's parents and sister. After the flood, we began to talk seriously about a target date for making the move. Kay said she would agree to move as soon as we adopted one more child. I said, "Well, if you can arrange it by next year, go ahead, but I don't think you can do it."

I should have known better. Kay went to see her doctor and told him we were looking to adopt another baby. Within a few days, he told her that there would be a baby coming in March 1968, and if she wanted the baby, he would work it out. That's how we got our fourth child, Christie, our wonderful blue-eyed, blonde, curly-haired, baby daughter.

In the months leading up to Christie's birth, we started making plans to leave Alaska permanently. In January, I finished up my schoolwork; I did not register for the spring. Christie was born in March, and 30 days after her birth, we had our first adoption hearing for her. In the normal process, there is a second and final hearing a year after the first, giving the biological parents an opportunity to change their minds before the adoption is made final. I warned Kay that we might be restricted in traveling before Christie's adoption was finalized, but she remained confident that all would be well.

When we went in for the adoption hearing, the judge wanted us to bring all the kids — the whole family — to the hearing. Kay and I testified, of course. The biological parents were not there. The judge was someone I had known since I was on the police department. He knew that we planned to leave Alaska, so he just asked if we would come back if the second hearing was required. When we told him we would, he said, "Then you're free to go." We now had our four children and we finalized our plans to leave Alaska permanently to go to Arkansas.

We sold the Telco Answering Service as well as our small private investigation and process serving business that we had run out of Telco. I resigned from Bob Parish's firm, with some sadness. Considering the business that I was in, I think he gave me even more of an education than the university did. What I learned from Bob I have used throughout the rest of my career.

I bought a new car for the move and a trailer to transport the valuables we would take with us. We sold everything else, loaded up the car and trailer, and on May 10, 1968, we left Alaska, headed south to make a new start in Arkansas.

Instead of heading straight to Arkansas, we planned to make a family trip of it, taking about three weeks. I had a brother who was in Detroit, so we stopped there to visit him and his family for a couple of days. Then we made a stop at Niagara Falls just for fun on the way to visit another brother and his family in Connecticut.

When we finally headed southwest, we made a few more stops along the way. I had seen many of the places we would travel through, but Kay had not, and of course neither had the kids. We spent a day sightseeing in New York City, visited an old classmate of mine in Pennsylvania, and did some more sightseeing in Washington, D.C.

We arrived at my mother's home in Arkansas on Memorial Day weekend, and were immediately welcomed with a huge family gathering hosted by my brother, Cecil. We were home at last.

Chapter 5

Back in Arkansas

WHEN WE ARRIVED in Arkansas, I was sure I could find work, but I did not have specific plans. I tried a couple of things — we even took an option to buy a small farm — but although we loved the farm life, I needed more to support my family.

I thought I was done with investigative work when I left Alaska, but it turned out the private investigation business was not done with me. Kay and I considered our options and decided that I would try to get work as a private investigator. Since Warren was so small, I decided to target the town of El Dorado, about 20 miles away.

That was the start of Fred Myers Investigations, later known as Myers Investigations. With Kay's help, I marketed my services first to the attorneys in El Dorado, then to those in the surrounding towns in South Arkansas. I would send marketing letters and then make personal calls to follow up. The experience I had gained in Alaska served me well as I began to get a wide variety of cases. I investigated auto accidents, product liability incidents, airplane accidents, missing persons — almost any type of case imaginable. Throughout my years owning Myers Investigations, I would conduct or supervise over 2,000 private investigations.

Within a few days, I had my first case from Brown, Compton, and Pruit, a local attorney's office, in which I successfully located a missing witness to an auto accident. The law firm that gave me that case, in late 1968, is still a client of our firm, more than 50 years later.

As the business started to take hold, we decided to buy a house and move our family to El Dorado. We set up a business office in the back room of our house, and soon I had more work than I could handle. Our nephew Ronnie Rand had just returned from Vietnam, where he had served as a Green Beret, and was looking for work, so I took him on to help with both paperwork and investigations.

In early 1969, I received a case that would have a great impact on our whole family. The attorney who gave me the case was Henry Woods, a partner in a Little Rock firm named McMath, Leatherman and Woods. McMath was a former governor of Arkansas, and Woods was known as one of the best trial lawyers in the state. He would later become a federal judge.

Woods hired me to find a witness whose testimony was vital to his case. Others had tried to locate him with no success. With Kay's help, I found the witness, interviewed him, and secured a statement from him, all within 24 hours. When I reported back to Henry Woods, he not only complimented my work, but suggested I move to Little Rock, where their firm was located. He assured me that if I did so, I could expect to receive regular work from them.

Kay and I talked it over and decided the promise of regular work from such a prominent law firm would make the move worthwhile, so in September 1969, we moved to Little Rock, rented a home, and settled in. I was 33 years old and had a wife and four children, Ellen was 13, Lee was 6, Katy was 3, and Christie was 2. Our family grew up in Little Rock and in June 1975, we welcomed our fifth child, Andy.

Since Little Rock is about 120 miles from El Dorado, I almost had to start from scratch in building my private investigation business. I started out in partnership with another investigations and security professional, but after only a few months, it became clear that we needed to part ways. I sold my share of the partnership — by agreement, taking my private investigation clients with me — and in April 1970 I established my new firm, Myers, Rand, and Associates, with Kay. In setting up the new firm, I offered our nephew Ronnie a partnership, and we hired Mel Fry as an investigator. We added a courier service, and Kay helped in the office whenever she could.

With my existing clients, and ongoing referrals from the McMath firm, the business slowly started to build. One of those existing clients was the Eilbott and Smith firm in Pine Bluff. Just a few days after opening the doors on our new firm, I took a call from one of their attorneys, Don Smith. That one call turned out to be life-changing. It would lead to the biggest case of my career and put our business on the map in extraordinary ways.

Our family was complete with the birth of baby Andy in 1975.

Chapter 6

A Fateful Phone Call

IT WAS MAY 10, 1970. I was in my office in Little Rock when I received that call from Don Smith, an attorney with the law firm of Reinberger, Eilbott, Smith and Staten in Pine Bluff. The firm handled both civil and criminal cases; I had been doing regular work for them for several months.

Don told me he represented Linda Shibley, a Pine Bluff schoolteacher and mother of two children. Linda was divorced from Sol Shibley and had been awarded legal custody of their two children, Kenny, age six, and Nofa, age four.

About ten days earlier, Linda's ex-husband, Sol, had come to Pine Bluff from his home in Tulsa. Exercising his court-awarded four-hour visitation rights, Sol told Linda he was taking the children to the city park. He left with the children, but never returned. Linda had searched the park, then filed a missing persons' report with the Pine Bluff Police. She then drove to Tulsa, where she learned that Sol had never returned to his apartment in Tulsa nor returned to his job at Texaco, where he worked as a petroleum engineer. Linda feared he had perhaps left the country with the children.

I went to Pine Bluff to meet with Don Smith and Linda Shibley, and was hired to locate the children. I was given a $1,000 retainer, and I immediately went to work on the case.

Linda provided all the background information she could on Sol, the children, and herself. I took notes of the entire history of their courtship, marriage, and the problems that led to their divorce. Linda gave me photos of the children and letters that Sol had written since their separation. This gave me the basic information I needed to start the investigation.

While Linda was a student at Ouachita Baptist University, a Christian university supported by the Southern Baptist Convention, she met a fellow student, Sol Shibley, a Palestinian. Sol was about 12 years old in 1947, when the First Arab-Israeli War broke out. In November 1947, the United Nations adopted a resolution partitioning what had been British Palestine into an Arab state and a Jewish state, with a special international regime around the holy cities of Jerusalem and Bethlehem. In the aftermath, tensions between the two sides erupted into war. Sol told Linda that one night the Jews busted into his home and blew his dad's head off as he watched. When he was 18 and had graduated from high school in what had become the state of Israel, his family helped him travel to the United States.

Sol was very intelligent. He was college material but did not have the funds to go to college. He had grown up Muslim, but he converted to Christianity and started making speeches in Christian churches about his past life and what it meant to now be a Christian. Soon, Sol had a scholarship to Ouachita Baptist University, where he and Linda became classmates. Linda, a devout Baptist and a member of the Immanuel Baptist Church in Pine Bluff, was impressed by Sol's devotion to the Christian faith, his intelligence, and his tragic upbringing. They were married after they both graduated, she as a teacher and he was a petroleum engineer.

At first, the young couple lived and worked in North Little Rock. Sol then got a great job with Texaco in Tulsa, Oklahoma, so they moved there and lived in Tulsa for about three years.

They had two children, Kenny, who was born in 1964, and Nofa, born two years later.

Linda said the trouble started in their marriage when Sol's personality began to change. He became sullen and appeared depressed. He decided to revert back to the Muslim religion of his youth and rejected the Christian faith. He told Linda that the children, Kenny and Nofa, would be raised in the Muslim faith. Linda said no and stood firm. Linda said that Sol held to a radical interpretation of Islam, believing that women are chattel, owned by their husbands. In his view, the husband was the absolute master and the wife must do whatever he wanted her to do. He believed the father had absolute rule over the children and could overrule anything the mother said or taught.

During this time, Sol was also arrested and charged with window peeping at a neighbor's home. His sentence included court-ordered psychiatric treatment. Linda filed for divorce, but before doing so, she moved back to Pine Bluff with the children. She got a job as a teacher in the Pine Bluff School District and established residence in Jefferson County, Arkansas. This meant that the jurisdiction controlling custody of the children was Jefferson County Chancery Court. During the ensuing custody battle, Linda reported that Sol had told her she would never raise his children — they would die first. Linda was granted custody and Sol was given visitation every other weekend, which included four hours of private time where he could take them to eat, to the park, shopping, etc. Linda told me that she begged the court to require every visit be monitored, but the court gave him four hours visitation alone anyway, with an admonishment not to abuse the privilege.

On the last Saturday of April, Linda prepared the children for their visit with Sol. He drove down from Tulsa and picked them up from Linda at her grandmother's house on West 17th. He told her he was taking them to the city park for a picnic and to play, and that he would be back in four hours, about 5:00 p.m.

At 5:00 p.m., Sol and the children did not return. Linda waited another half hour, then drove to the city park. She spoke with several people in the park, but no one had seen Sol or the children. Linda then went to the police, who refused to take a missing persons' report for at least 24 hours because the children were with their father, even though he was violating the child custody decree. Linda called her attorney, Don Smith, and advised him what had happened.

By the next day, Linda still had not heard anything. She drove around the area, checking the motels, but found nothing. On Monday morning, she requested a few days off from the school district and filed a missing persons' report with the police. She then drove to Tulsa and went to Sol's employer, Texaco. There she was told that Sol was expected back at work that day, but he had not come in and he had not requested time off. Linda went to Sol's apartment. She could not get in and saw no sign that Sol had returned since leaving on Saturday morning.

Linda spent several days in Tulsa, thinking Sol would return there to his job and apartment with the children, but he never appeared. Her mother and grandmother in Pine Bluff monitored the phone. Sol never called Linda or his employer. Linda returned to Pine Bluff and contacted Sol's family in Israel, who had not heard from Sol either. She returned to teaching for the month left in the school year while I began my search for Kenny and Nofa Shibley.

Chapter 7

Building the Case

WHEN I STARTED my search for Kenny and Nofa Shibley in 1970, I had just opened a new private investigation business — Myers, Rand & Associates — in partnership with my nephew Ronnie Rand. Our fledgling business, that was only a few weeks old, would be challenged beyond our wildest expectations with the aftermath of getting this investigation. By the time the Shibleys entered my life, I had been doing private investigation for seven years, but this case was something else.

Whenever I took an assignment, I tried to pull every bit of information I could from the client. I would carefully try to determine what the client wanted to accomplish through my investigation. I would ask the client for suggestions, but was always careful to say that I couldn't promise to get the results they wanted. I would promise to do the best job I could do — as long as it was legal — to try and accomplish what they wanted. I spent a lot of time reading, studying, and talking to people. I joined professional organizations and read their publications. I went to seminars when I could afford it. I talked to other people in the business. I went to the courthouse and sat in on trials and watched how attorneys presented evidence. I learned more about the difference between civil cases and the criminal cases I had worked on while a police officer in Fairbanks.

One of the things I learned is that every case is unique. Every case must be studied, planned, and investigated according to the needs of that specific case as no two cases are alike. Every case was especially important when it came to me; it was one of the most important issues in the life of the client who hired me. If not, they would not hire me. I took every case I ever had very seriously — perhaps more than I should have. That was the drive I brought to the Shibley case.

Armed with all the information I had gathered and a plan for the investigation, I first went to Tulsa with our investigator, Mel Fry. With the cooperation of the landlord, we checked the apartment, and it was evident Sol had not returned there after picking up the children; it was as if he just left for the weekend. His mailbox had mail sticking out of it just far enough to see the names of some credit card companies which might give us a lead. We developed all the information we could in Tulsa and returned to Little Rock.

Through interviews, phone calls, and records research, we received cooperation from people who had access to credit card records. With the help of those records, we quickly learned that two days after Sol and the children left Pine Bluff, he had used his Sears credit card to purchase new clothes, personal items, and luggage for himself and the children from a Sears in Louisville, Kentucky. From motor vehicle records in Oklahoma, we obtained registration information and title information on his vehicle and learned that an application for a new title had been made.

We traced the new title application to a used car dealer in Detroit, Michigan and learned that Sol had sold his car to a dealer for cash at a wholesale price two days after he left Kentucky. We learned that he and the children had taken a bus from Detroit to Toronto, Canada. We were not sure why he had sold his car. We knew he had some money, but not a great deal of it.

Regardless, based on the fact that Sol had not returned the children to their mother as the custody order required and on the evidence we had developed that he had taken the children out of the state, we obtained a warrant in Jefferson County for felony child custody violation.

Kenny Shibley   *Nofa Shibley*

We had learned that Sol had purchased tickets for himself and the children to fly from Toronto to Paris, so we went to the federal authorities and requested that they issue an unlawful flight felony warrant for Sol as well. Copies of such warrants were not usually given to private investigators, but exceptions were made in this case with the influence and assistance of judicial and prosecuting officials in Jefferson County, who had been involved in this case from the start.

For a while, the trail ended in Paris. Working mostly by phone, I attempted to develop leads of where Sol Shibley had gone from there, but the trail had gone cold.

It was time to regroup. We had used the initial $1,000 retainer and Don Smith had told me from the beginning neither he nor his law firm would be responsible for additional fees or expenses. From this point forward, the Shibley family would be responsible for any further investigation and expenses in this case.

I had a meeting with Linda and her mother, Betty Short, in Mrs. Short's home in White Hall, just south of Little Rock. Mrs. Short told me she wanted me to continue working on the case, and she assured me she would be personally responsible to pay all fees and expenses. She said, "You find those children and bring them home and I will pay you in full, even if I have to sell my home to do it."

In those days, I still operated on a verbal promise and a handshake. I never bothered with written contracts then and for the most part, I seldom have. Mrs. Short paid me another $1,000 retainer to apply toward fees and expenses. She told me, with her daughter's confirmation, that there was $3,000 left in a trust for Linda from her deceased father's insurance, which they would close out and use for the investigation. Beyond that, Mrs. Short and her husband would pay my fees.

We agreed that my fee would be $12 per hour and $0.15 per auto mile plus out of pocket expenses. When I worked out of town overnight, the fee was a flat $100 per day plus expenses, regardless of the number of hours for each day. Mrs. Short agreed to those fees and expenses.

At that time, we did have other work in our firm. Ronnie and I had just one full-time paid employee, Mel Fry. He was our field investigator, and we had plenty of work to keep him busy, mostly working on fraudulent insurance claims and other missing person cases. Ronnie was responsible for the office work, assisted by Kay when she could come in and help him. He and I agreed that I would do all of the work on the Shibley case and help out on anything else I had time for, including managing our small, practically new business. It was a lot for him to handle, since Ronnie was not only a new business owner, but also a newlywed. He had recently married Mary Lynn Johnson, the sister of Tommy Johnson who, with his wife Bernice, were Kay's and my next door neighbors and close friends.

When I was gone, Ronnie would manage the business and do investigative work as much as possible. Kay would help him in the office as available, but she still had to take care of our four young children at home.

I continued my efforts to trace down and find Kenny and Nofa Shibley. In early July, I learned that a New York firm had run a credit check on Sol Shibley about six months earlier. When I contacted the company, I was told that the purpose of the credit check was confidential and they could not tell me anything, but I was not deterred. As is my custom in following leads where I need information badly, I started working my way up the management chain of the company, explaining to each person with whom I spoke why I was seeking the information. Finally, I found a sympathetic supervisor, who agreed to give me information off the record.

He told me the credit check had been run as part of a background investigation for possible employment with the Oasis Oil Company of Libya. At last, a lead — not certain, but a positive lead to follow. I already had my passport — a private investigator should always keep a current passport — so I immediately applied for a visa to Libya and told Linda to do the same.

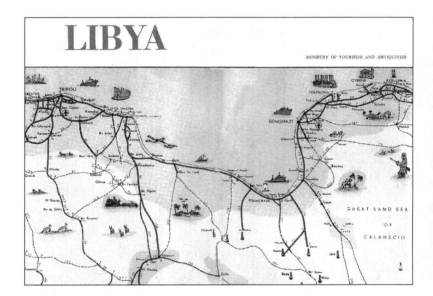

Chapter 8

Off to Libya

LIBYA IS A LARGE COUNTRY in North Africa, with the north bordering the Mediterranean Sea, the east bordering Egypt, and the west bordering Tunisia and Algeria. South of Libya are other African countries; north, across the Mediterranean are Italy, the island of Crete, and Greece; northeast is Israel.

I knew from news reports that there had been a recent revolution in Libya. A 29-year-old Libyan military officer named Col. Muammar al-Qaddafi had led a group of military officers and troops, overthrowing King Idres and his government. King Idres' government had been friendly to the United States as the United States had maintained a large Air Force base near Libya's capital city of Tripoli since World War II, when our military fought there to liberate Libya from Italy and Germany. Col. al-Qaddafi, however, installed military rule, and quickly developed communist ties. He took over the U. S. airbase and did the same with the British Airbase near Benghazi. He expelled all American and British military, and was moving against other governments as well as civilian companies and corporations that had interests in the country.

Americans were heavily invested in Libyan oil exploration and oil production; much of the modern technology was still controlled by American oil companies. This investment lead to the U.S. still having a strong commercial interest there, even though the military had been booted out of Libya. America also still had an ambassador in Tripoli and a consulate office in Benghazi, the two largest cities in Libya.

As previously mentioned, Sol Shibley had grown up in Palestine. In the aftermath of the Arab-Israeli wars and the establishment of the state of Israel, many Palestinians had fled the country. Some were living in nearby Arab countries, like Libya, Jordan, Egypt, and others. Under Col. al-Qaddafi, Libya had offered Libyan citizenship to all Palestinians who came there and declared Libya their home.

I knew that Sol, with a degree in petroleum engineering and several years' experience with Texaco, would be very welcome in Libya, especially with oil production being their major industry. Before I committed to traveling there myself, I devised a plan to try to determine if Sol and the children had gone to Libya. I contacted the U.S. State Department and requested a list of attorneys in Libya who did business with or represented our government's interests there, as well as American oil company interests. I received a list of about ten Libyan attorneys and law firms, and I began calling those firms.

I first asked for someone who could speak English, then told them I needed to know if Sol Shibley and his children had entered the country. A law firm in Tripoli said they could help me; they had a connection with Libyan immigration and could get the names if they were there. We were to wire them a $2,000 retainer, which Betty Short did. About four days later, the lawyer called with news. He told me that Sol and the children had arrived in Libya about June 15, but that Sol had not gone to work at the Oasis Oil Company of Libya. They had not been able to find any record of Sol leaving Libya, so he might still be in the country.

I informed Linda, and we prepared to leave for Libya immediately. Betty Short provided me an expense advance of $5,000. I left about half of the money with Ronnie and Kay and used my American Express card to buy plane tickets for Linda and me.

On July 27, 1970, Linda and I left Little Rock and flew to New York, then across the Atlantic to Lisbon, Portugal, and then on to Rome, Italy. Since we had a night and day in Rome before our flight to Libya, we checked into a hotel and took advantage of the time to see a few of the sights. Linda and I took a guided tour of the city. The next morning, we got an English-speaking cabdriver to take us to the Vatican, where we toured St Peter's Basilica, one of the largest church buildings in the world. We visited the Sistine Chapel and saw Michelangelo's beautiful paintings. We then went to the San Pietro in Vincoli, where there is a set of shackles which they claim are the actual chains worn by Paul, Christ's disciple, when he was in prison. There was an earthquake and the chains were loosened, freeing him. We also went to see the remains of the Coliseum and arena.

Our Libyan Arab National Airlines flight left Rome for Libya about 7:00 p.m. that evening. We boarded and flew to Tripoli, arriving about 9:30 p.m. The airport where we landed had been the U.S. airbase until a few months earlier but was now controlled by the Libyan military. The military was standing around everywhere, holding automatic rifles, and were anything but friendly.

When we approached customs, they looked at our passports and visas, and then turned our suitcases upside down, dumping everything out, scattering our belongings and searching them. Linda and I were both patted down. They then stamped our visas and passports. We had to repack our suitcases; nothing was replaced for us. We walked down the line of taxis asking if anyone spoke English until one cab driver said yes, then we got in and told him to take us to a good hotel. He took us to the nicest hotel in town called the Grand Tripoli Hotel.

On the way to the hotel, the driver, Khaled, told us that he had worked for the U.S. airbase in a civilian capacity. When the American military were kicked out of the country, he had been left without a job, so he just started driving a taxi. According to him, the hotel he took us to was the safest place to be in Libya. Khaled went in with us to discuss our rooms, rates, and more with the hotel clerk. He also took $100 in American money and exchanged it for Libyan money with the hotel office, as this was an official money exchange station. We tipped Khaled well and asked him to pick us up at eight the following morning and drive us around until noon. We got two hotel rooms and went to bed about midnight.

At 8 a.m., Khaled picked us up, and I asked that he first take us to the American Embassy. At the embassy, we met with a consular officer, who took us in to meet Ambassador Joseph Palmer. We told the two our story, and showed them the legal documents we had brought, including the custody papers and the warrants for Sol Shibley. Ambassador Palmer and the consular officer advised us that all legal decisions in Libya were made under Libyan law; any decision outside of that would be made for some other reason, perhaps political. We were cautioned not to break any Libyan laws, as the officials would be very harsh on us, and the U.S. government could not protect us. We would not be afforded the same rights we would have back in the United States.

We were reminded to make sure that no one misunderstood the professional relationship between Linda and myself. An unmarried couple in Libya caught committing adultery could be punished by death under Islamic law, which is enforced whenever they want to. We were warned that our hotel rooms would probably be bugged with recording devices, and nothing we said in our hotel rooms would likely be private. We were advised to keep in close contact with the American authorities, although they did not know how long they would be there. The embassy staff were at risk of being told to leave the country at any time; the Libyan government were expected to confiscate all oil company assets.

We asked the consular officer at the American Embassy about our hotel and were told that it was the best and safest place for an American in Libya at that time. We were reminded that the Libyan government of King Idres, which was friendly to Americans, had just been overthrown. The new revolutionary government of Col. Muammar al-Qaddafi was not friendly to the American government or to Americans in general. Qaddafi's government was moving slowly against the foreign governments who had embassies there and closing them down. The American military and the British military had already been kicked out of Libya, and the Libyans had already taken over the U.S. airbase in Tripoli and the British airbase in Benghazi. However, the diplomatic corps (embassies, ambassadors, consular officers and staff) still remained at that time. There were also several American oil companies still operating in the exploration and production of Libyan oil.

I asked if someone would write out for me or provide me with the Arabic numbers zero through nine, so I could study and figure out the Arabic money we would be using while we were there. Over the next few days, I spent quite a lot of time studying those numbers and comparing them with the numbers on the Libyan money, coins, street signs, numbers on buildings, newspaper pages, menus, etc., until I could recognize and remember them.

When we left the embassy, we took the taxi to the office of the attorney I had hired while I was still in Arkansas. A principal attorney in the firm was a Palestinian named Ibrahim Bezbazet, who met with us to discuss the case. His firm had represented American interests there in the past, including American oil companies, and had been referred to me by the U.S. Department of State. They confirmed for us that Sol, Kenny, and Nofa Shibley were in Libya.

Ibrahim Bezbazet agreed to represent our interests there, requiring an additional $3,000 deposit towards his time and expenses. I liked him immediately — he impressed me as a competent attorney. He told me that he had been educated in England and France. After returning to Libya, he had taken a refresher in Libyan law, passed the bar and got his license. He had worked for this law firm for about four years, representing mostly American companies, government, and individual interests. He explained the difference between family law in Libya and in the United States, particularly regarding divorce and child custody issues.

Based on my own previous research, I understood that Libya was basically an Islamic country and Libyan law was primarily based on the Quran and Islamic sharia law. Under those teachings, the male head of the household was strongly favored in almost all family court matters. The man could marry and have multiple wives at the same time. I was told that a man could divorce any wife at will by simply saying "I divorce you" three times, then spitting on the ground and to finalize the divorce. I would later learn that this was not necessarily the case. However, the children were given to the man in almost all cases.

It would be extremely difficult — borderline unheard of — for children to be taken from a father who wanted them and was caring for them. This case further complicated by the fact that even though Sol Shibley was raised in Israel, he was

Palestinian by birth, while Linda was a Caucasian American. He had also renounced his Christian faith and re-embraced the Islamic faith. Linda was a Christian, a Baptist. These were all obstacles we were warned about in the first interview.

There was one very touchy subject I felt needed to be addressed with Bezbazet. I was quite aware of the strong differences between the Palestinians and Christians in their political and religious opinions. Yet, apart from that, Bezbazet seemed the most qualified and best legal help we could hire there. I decided before we made the final decision to approach this directly. I reminded him that Sol Shibley was, to him, a fellow Palestinian, while he would be representing a female Christian against Sol in a court that would traditionally favor the male Palestinian on the issues with which we were dealing.

Mr. Bezbazet told me that if he took our case, he would set aside all political and personal religious considerations in which he and Sol Shibley might share a common position. He would do the best he could to recover Linda's children for her, though he acknowledged it would be an uphill battle.

Linda and I talked privately. A major consideration was that Mr. Bezbazet spoke fluent English, so we could communicate. We agreed that hiring Bezbazet seemed the logical way to go, so Linda asked me to give him a $3,000 check. She said she would wire her mother to give Kay a $3,000 check to put in our bank account to cover that expense, which she did.

Ibrahim Bezbazet offered to take us to a late lunch at a typical Libyan restaurant, and we agreed. We drove to a crowded restaurant which he said was mostly patronized by business and professional people. He recommended a popular Libyan dish to us. When the food came, it looked like a bowl of stew, with hard-crusted bread on the side. I asked about the stew, and he told me it was camel meat, their most common meat.

It tasted like tough, strong beef. For himself, Bezbazet ordered an American-style hamburger and fries. I wished I had done the same.

Even though the lunch was entertaining, we still had to locate Sol Shibley. We knew that before he had arrived, he had the offer of a job with the Oasis Oil Company of Libya, which was a subsidiary of the Occidental Petroleum Company of America. Bezbazet assigned a young Libyan law clerk, Tareq, from his office to work with me as a guide, driver and interpreter. Tareq was only 19 or 20 and spoke broken English but, with effort, we could understand one another. We knew that we would be severely handicapped when we wanted and needed information from Libyans, but felt using him to make inquiries for us would give us a much better chance of success. We then continued our investigation in Libya to locate Sol and the children.

We learned that upon Sol's arrival over a month earlier, he had reported to the Tripoli office of the Oasis Oil Company of Libya. However, he had made a mistake by entering Libya on a tourist visa instead of a work visa. The company, being American-owned, refused to put him to work, since hiring a tourist would have been a violation of the law. Through our inquiries we learned that the new revolutionary government had issued a policy directive that any Palestinian who held foreign citizenship would be granted citizenship in Libya if they denounced their other citizenship. Sol had his original Israeli citizenship, and he had also become a U.S. citizen.We asked the Bezbazet law firm to check with the Libyan immigration authorities and try to determine if he had accepted Libyan citizenship. If he had, we could assume he was still in Libya, working somewhere. If he had not, he had probably moved on, perhaps to Israel where his mother and other family members still lived.

Once the records were checked at the Immigration Office, we learned that he had denounced his Israeli and American citizenships, and had accepted the Libyan citizenship offered to Palestinians, declaring himself a Palestinian refugee.

We began a search for his new employer, and within a few days we learned that Sol was working for the Libyan government as a petroleum engineer, stationed out of Benghazi. Benghazi, with a population of about 600,000, was the second largest city in Libya, next to Tripoli with its population of about 1 million. Much of the rest of the country was rural desert, with small towns and villages dotting the countryside.

After discussing this latest information with Ibrahim Bezbazet, we agreed that we needed to go to the city of Benghazi and work from there. Bezbazet referred us to an attorney in Benghazi, Ali Buhidma. We would have to hire Buhidma separately, but Bezbazet said he would contact him, tell him about us, and brief him on our case. Ali Buhidma would help us with our legal needs in Benghazi. Bezbazet also said that if it were necessary at any time, he would fly over and assist. He told us to call him any time about any questions we might have.

Chapter 9

On to Benghazi

BENGHAZI IS LOCATED about 600 miles east of Tripoli and about 100 miles west of the Egyptian border. Both cities are situated on the northern edge of Libya, on the coast of the Mediterranean Sea.

Ten days after we arrived in Libya, during the first week of August, we flew from Tripoli to Benghazi on Libyan National Airlines. The only daily flight left in the late afternoon, made one stop about midway, and landed in Benghazi about 9:00 p.m. Upon arrival, as we had in Tripoli, we went outside to the line of taxi cabs parked at the curb. I walked down the row, asking if any driver spoke English, and finally, one driver said he did.

We got in and asked him to take us to a downtown hotel. He took us to the Benghazi Hotel, a very modern hotel on the edge of town, but they were full for the night. The cab driver, Hamza, told us there were a lot of oil workers in town who were leaving the country. He then took us to a small hotel downtown which he said the English called the Lincoln Hotel, though it had a different Arabic name. On the way, Hamza asked us our business, and I showed him a picture of Sol and the two children. I told Hamza why we were searching for them, and that Linda was the children's mother.

When we arrived at the hotel, Hamza went inside and helped us check in, since the desk clerk did not speak English. We were told only a few rooms at the hotel had air conditioning, even though this appeared to be the most modern — and perhaps the newest — hotel in Benghazi. We were given two rooms on the third floor. There were no elevators, so Hamza helped us take our luggage to our rooms. After I tipped him, he said, "Let's go down to the desk clerk and see if he has seen Mr. Shibley and the children."

I had no hope of that accomplishing anything. After all, this was a town of 600,000, and finding them this way would be like finding the proverbial needle in a haystack. Hamza took the photos to the desk clerk with me following him. It was now about 10:00 p.m. He showed the desk clerk the photos and they conversed in Arabic.

What happened next is almost unbelievable. It was as if we found the needle in the first handful of straw we plucked from the haystack. It was a miracle! While looking at the photos, the clerk, an Arab about 25 years of age, started waving his arms and pointing up. Hamza turned to me and said, "The clerk says they are upstairs, and he gave us the room number."

Acting as an interpreter, Hamza told me there were no elevators and that the back stairs were sealed off at night. Therefore, there was only one way out and that was down the stairs by the lobby. The desk clerk told us that Sol went to work each morning and took the children to a daycare somewhere. I tipped the desk clerk with $20 in American cash, and the cab driver with $40.

I felt then, and I have always felt since, that God led me to Shibley and the children in a town that size. It could have taken me a month or more to find them, especially working in a foreign country with the language and cultural barriers.

Linda and I sat down to consider our strategy. Unbelievably, we were in a hotel with Sol and the children and he did not know we were there. In my briefcase was a warrant issued for him in Arkansas. If we had been anywhere in the United States, I could have called the police. However, Libya and the United States had no extradition treaty. I knew the police would not help us. In fact, because of their legal system, they would probably favor Mr. Shibley. We had not yet had an opportunity to contact the local lawyer to get legal advice, and had not even had an opportunity to check in with the local consulate office in Benghazi, which I had planned to do the next morning.

Linda could barely contain her emotions. She had not seen her children since they had been abducted three months earlier; and we were now within 100 feet of them. She was crying some and almost hyperventilating. To do nothing would probably mean that Sol Shibley would be told we were there, and he and the children would disappear, making it extremely hard to find them again.

I knew Sol was working for the government, but I did not know exactly where. Anything we did would be a rough calculated risk. Linda agreed that I should make the decision, because she was in no emotional state to tell me what she thought I should do. I knew if I made the wrong decision, she might never see her children again. That weighed heavily on me, and we prayed together.

I decided I should go to Sol's room alone to confront him. I planned out exactly what I would do and say when confronting him. Although I had never met him personally, I knew quite a lot about him. I had seen pictures of him and read the letters he had sent to Linda and the children after the separation. The letters told me that he was smart and cunning, but I suspected he was probably also a coward. However, his children and his pride were at stake, so I anticipated that he would act tough. I did not know exactly what to expect, but I figured this approach was better than doing nothing or taking a chance on waiting until the next day.

I thought of Kay and our four children back home. Ronnie was handling the business with Kay's help. I knew money was tight. I had talked with Kay on the phone at least once since I had been in Libya, but there were no phones in the hotel rooms. To make a long-distance call, we had to go to a telephone company office and fill out an application. On the application, we had to state who we were, who we were calling, and why. We had to stand in line to turn in the application and be interviewed, then we had to sit and wait for the call to be put through. This whole process to make the call usually took three or four hours. We had to pay cash for the calls, and although I do not remember the exact cost, my recollection is that it was $20 to $30 for a 15-minute call.

Because calls were so difficult and expensive, much of my communication with home was by telegram and letters. When I did call, I tried to coordinate it so that Ronnie could be with Kay and the children so we could discuss the business a little. We also used Western Union telegrams to communicate, since those messages could be brief, to the point, and much less expensive. We usually sent telegrams once or twice a week.

Kay would write long letters full of news and the day-to-day doings — often signed, "Your lonesome wife" — but these were no substitute for being home with my family. The separation was hard on all of us, compounded by the tension of my being so far away, in such a dangerous place. I wrote almost every day, but sometimes would write a long letter over two or three days and mail it all at once to Kay, as well as mailing postcards to the children.

If I were successful in this case, it had been agreed that I would be paid $100 per day plus expenses. My motive at that point was much more about recovering the children than about money, but the money was important. We needed it for our business and our family — if I did not get paid on this case it could be a financial disaster for both. However, I was determined to succeed, not only for the sake of the children, but also for the money I would earn, and the professional and personal satisfaction I would receive.

With the federal "unlawful flight" warrant and the Arkansas felony warrant for violation of a child custody order in my pocket, I walked up to Sol's door and knocked. It was about 10:30 p.m. I heard him ask who was there, and I replied, "Fred Myers, from Little Rock, Arkansas." He cracked open the door about three inches and I saw him for the first time.

"What do *you* want?"

I told Sol I wanted to talk with him for a few minutes, and that I thought it was in the best interest of everyone involved.

I was concerned that he might have a gun. Sol was a Palestinian who, I had been told, had already joined the Palestinian Liberation Organization (PLO). I knew he could have a gun if he wanted to have one, but I had to try. I told him I was a private investigator from Little Rock, that I had a felony warrant for his arrest, and that Linda was in the hotel. I also told him that if he would let Linda have the children, I would not give the warrant to the authorities to serve, that we would just take the children and go home.

Sol replied that the warrant was no good in Libya and that Libya would not recognize it. He also rebutted with, "You and Linda had better leave now. I've got friends in the PLO, and if I call them, you both will disappear."

He had probably checked the warrant's legality out before he came to Libya. I knew the organization he mentioned was a well-known and highly organized terrorist organization under the leadership of Yasser Arafat. If Sol had truly joined the Palestinian Liberation Organization, which was protected and welcomed in Libya, I knew we could be in danger as any action taken against us would receive little or no negative reaction from the Libyan authorities.

I then asked Sol if Linda could just see the children, since she was downstairs and had not seen them in three months. He growled, "Leave, both of you, or you will wish you had." He slammed the door shut and I heard him attach the chain lock.

I walked back downstairs and discussed with Linda what had transpired. I had learned that the only exit from the three floors upstairs was down the stairs that led to the lobby, where we were seated, and out the front door. The back stairs and door were locked and blocked off. This would serve as an advantage to us, because if Sol or the children tried to leave, we would at least be aware of it.

I encouraged Linda to go to her room and get some rest. I would sit in the lobby throughout the night and wait for Mr. Shibley or the children to attempt to leave the hotel. Linda did go upstairs for a short time, but soon came back to the lobby, saying she could not sleep and would wait with me. She also said she did not want to risk missing a chance to see her children when they did come out. We ended up staying in the lobby all night. About 5:00 a.m., people began to come and go, up and down the stairs. Of course, we could not see if they were going to the room occupied by Sol, Kenny, and Nofa, but I suspected some were going to that room. We waited and watched.

At about 6:00 a.m., Sol walked down the stairs and Linda and I stood up. Sol immediately started waving his arms and yelling, "What are you doing here? You will be sorry! Go, today, back to America." He told us if we did not leave, we would be arrested. I told him that the authorities here would not be pleased with what he had done, but if he would simply let Linda have the children, we would leave and not report anything. Sol laughed and began speaking in Arabic, which of course we did not understand. A crowd had started to gather around us, and I suspected he was appealing to them.

Suddenly, a man jumped up onto my back, locking his legs and feet around my waist and an arm under my neck and chin, in a hammerlock fashion. This surprised me and I started to pitch him off by bending forward. At that moment, Sol punched me in the face with his fist.

Sol was screaming in Arabic, and the other people in the crowd were becoming excited. Linda started screaming, "Stop, please stop!" I defended myself from Sol's repeated blows and successfully pitched the other man over my head onto the floor.

At that moment, two women came running down the stairs, carrying Kenny and Nofa. Three or four men were with them, probably as guards. Linda began screaming the children's names and trying to get to them, but she was hampered by the crowd. However, the children saw her and started screaming, "Mommy, Mommy!"

The two women carrying the children ran into the street, followed by the men accompanying them, and disappeared into the crowd. I told Linda to calm down, and she collapsed into a chair, sobbing. Sol was still in my face, throwing an occasional punch, which l fended off, but never attempted to strike him back. I did not want any reason to be arrested and charged with fighting or assault. I knew I was at risk already, and Sol certainly had an advantage.

I grabbed Linda's hand and said, "Let's go." We went upstairs to our rooms and I said, "Let us get out of here as quickly as we can. I stand a high risk of being arrested for fighting or assault."

We had not unpacked our bags from the night before, so we grabbed them and went out to the street. We walked down the street until we could flag down a taxi. We had the address of the American Consulate in Benghazi, and our attorney in Tripoli had written out the address in Arabic. I showed it to the cab driver, and he drove us to the consulate. We were very relieved to get inside. We checked in with the desk, asked to see a consular officer, and were given a comfortable waiting area with coffee and snacks while we waited.

When the consular officer came in, we told him our story as he listened patiently. He told us that he had heard about us by a dispatch from the embassy in Tripoli and had been told that we might be coming to Benghazi. He offered all the help he could give us but cautioned us that there were some things the consulate's office could not do. He told us that the safest place to stay, outside of the American community where Americans rented homes, was the Benghazi Hotel. It was rather expensive, but was operated professionally, and most people from other countries stayed there. He cautioned us that the criminal code was strict and severely enforced. He also warned us that if we ran into problems with the Libyan government, there was little the consulate's office could do. We were reminded again that our hotel rooms would probably be bugged, and there was little we would do or say that Libyan officials would not know about.

The consular officer called in a communications officer to help us get settled. His name was Allan Largent, and he was about my age. The consular officer then asked Allan to take us to the Benghazi Hotel and get us checked in. Allan drove us to the hotel in an official car. We checked into our rooms, which were side by side on the third floor. We could step outside our doors and look over a rail down into the lobby area and the front desk. Our rooms were next door to each other and for some reason, there was a small solid window or shutter between the rooms, about two feet square. We could open the solid window, like a cabinet door, and communicate, and either side could lock it shut. When we were at the hotel, we mostly stayed in our own individual rooms, but occasionally, we would visit. Linda and I each had a small Bible with us, so we would have to do our worship in private, and occasionally had prayer together in our rooms — this was still a risk though due to Col. al-Qaddafi's ban on Christianity. When we did visit one another, we would leave the door ajar, so the hotel staff could look in on us anytime they wished to verify that we were not committing a capital offense in the form of adultery.

We told Allan we needed to see our new lawyer in Benghazi and get legal advice as to what to do next. It was important for us to have a cab driver we could talk to and who could interpret for us. I asked him to help us find a cab driver who could speak English, so he made a call and got a cab driver who served a lot of people from the Consulate's Office.

That afternoon, we took a cab downtown to the office of Ali Buhidma, our new attorney in Benghazi. Mr. Buhidma was a Libyan and had received a call from Bezbazet in Tripoli. I paid him the $2,000 retainer he required, and we reviewed the case with him. He was blunt in saying there was almost no chance of Linda getting the children through the Libyan court system. He gave us no encouragement but said he would represent Linda to the best of his ability, and we would just have to see where the case went. He asked me to draft out an affidavit of the history of the case, have it translated into Arabic, and attach to it all of the documents I had: divorce decree, the child custody award, and the warrant for Sol Shibley, and then return it to him to file.

We went back to the hotel and got to work. I drafted a history of the case and finished about midnight. The next morning, we took a cab to the consulate's office. Linda was with me as she was afraid to stay alone, even at the hotel. I asked the consulate staff to recommend a translator who could certify the translation for court filing. One of the staff escorted us to a nearby small office, where a man was introduced to us as a certified translator. We showed him the document, and after looking at it briefly, he told us that the translation would cost $250 in advance. I asked for assurance that the local courts would accept the translation and with his assurance that it would be translated and filed the following day, we paid him and returned to the consulate's office.

The consular officer told us he and his wife would like to host a social gathering at his official residence that evening, with Linda and me as guests. I learned this is one of the things they do as part of their duties as foreign officers. We were in a foreign and rather hostile country, and this was their way of bringing us into their small circle. At that point, it was obvious that even though I would dedicate every minute I could to constructive work on the case and the recovery of the children, I was going to have some extra time on my hands. Besides, it seemed that it might be helpful to get better acquainted with the people there, including the Americans, and learn how they moved around and got along.

Allan Largent and his wife, Carolyn, drove us to the reception that evening, where we met a group of about 30 people. About half of them were members of the Foreign Service as consulate employees and their spouses and staff. The others were Americans who worked there, mostly for oil companies. Most of the civilians had no family members nearby. All had been sent back to the States since the revolution a few months earlier when al-Qaddafi came into power.

Everyone seemed interested in our story and extended their sympathies to Linda; a few offered words of wisdom and advice. Most everyone cautioned me to be very careful in dealing with the courts and the government of Libya and to trust no one outside the American community. I learned that night that the civilian workers did not expect to be in the country much longer. It was expected that the Libyan revolutionary government would nationalize all American assets and bar all civilians from remaining in the country. They felt their tenure was to be short and that it was just a matter of time. This turned out to be true, for just a few months later, as Libya did nationalize and seize all American-owned assets. All Americans were expelled from the country, and diplomatic relations with Libya were severed. The situation continued for nearly 40 years, until the fall of the Qaddafi government in 2011.

At the gathering that night, I met another guest who was a manager with a major petroleum company. Having been in Libya with the company for several years, he was quite angry with his industry's situation. He felt sure that the Libyan government was about to take his company's assets but would wait until it was best for them. His company was heavily involved in oil exploration. Libya wanted the exploration to continue but lacked adequately trained engineers and technicians to do the needed work. Libya needed the American and other foreign-trained experts at the oil companies to do the work to make the exploration proceed smoothly.

As we were getting acquainted, the fact came out that I was a pilot as well as a private investigator. The oil company manager asked me about my experience and what I was qualified to fly. I told him I was licensed to fly single engine land and had taken training for commercial and instrument flying, but had never taken my tests for those certifications. My experience was mostly in Cessna 150s, 172s, and 180s, plus the Piper Cherokee 140, and Taylor Craft. I expect he checked me out a bit after that night.

The following day, we went back to the translator to pick up the case documents. Although we had been promised they would be ready, I learned they were almost half done. I also quickly learned that such a delay was typical. It proved to be the norm and custom there.

When we returned to the hotel, we were greeted with three police officers waiting for us. Two were armed with pistols and one had a rifle that I believed to be a M-16 Automatic. One of them showed us his ID and requested mine while telling me to come with them. While asking if I was under arrest, two of the officers pulled their pistols and ordered me to get into their Jeep.

I was then taken to the local police station, where I was interrogated. I was sat in a chair in the middle of a room with only a light shining on my head. Another officer joined the three that had brought me to the chamber, but two of the men were the main interrogators. The other men stood at my back with their guns pointed at me, one of which was pressed against the back of my head. They had asked me about my "friends" at the hotel and accused me of being a spy as well as being a part of the CIA. I told them the story of why I was in Libya, and they released me after roughly two hours. I walked back to the hotel, shaken.

Chapter 10

Going to Court

AFTER WE HAD BEEN in Benghazi about a week, we finally got the document translation. We took it to our lawyer, Mr. Buhidma, and he filed a petition with the local court requesting that the Libyan court honor the child custody decree given in the American courts and return the children to Linda Shibley. This petition also requested that the court take the children into protective custody until the case was decided, with Linda being permitted to visit them.

We were told that the court would consider our petition and we would receive a response in one week. The attorney did persuade the court to allow Linda a one-hour visit with the children. The visit was held at a day care center, under supervision. Sol was also at the facility, but Linda was allowed to see the children privately. I was in the waiting area with Sol Shibley, and attempted to talk with him, but he only snarled, made threats, and turned his back on me. I had hoped to appeal to him on behalf of the children, but all of my efforts fell on deaf ears.

Sol Shibley bragged to me that he was employed by the Libyan government as a petroleum engineer. He also told me that Libya was now his permanent home, that he had renounced his United States citizenship and had been granted Libyan citizenship. He also emphasized again that he was a member of the PLO, and they would do for him whatever he asked. My concerns, however, were drowned by the feeling of happiness for Linda being able to see her children.

At the end of the visit, I was able to meet Kenny and Nofa briefly. When we left, Linda was in tears but relieved to have seen and visited the children for the first time in over three months. Linda was helpful and left all decisions as to how to proceed up to me. She expressed optimism. I fully understood the difficult task we faced in attempting to recover the children and I never gave her any assurance that we would succeed, only that I would do my best and pray for just results.

The next hearing was scheduled on a Sunday, as were all further hearings on our case. I felt that schedule may have been purposeful, to show contempt for our holy day, the day we as Christians would normally worship. That Sunday, we went to the courthouse with our attorney for the second time.

The courthouse was interesting to me. It was a stone building, about four stories high, in the downtown area, and like many of our old courthouses in the United States. It was rather plain with narrow halls and small offices. There were no elevators that I saw, and no air conditioning. Even though Benghazi was a sizable city, most of the commercial buildings were block style, square, and appeared quite old.

Each trip to the courthouse — which happened almost every Sunday for three months — would be an all-day event. We would arrive before 8:00 a.m., meet our lawyer, Mr. Buhidma, then be asked to wait in a small room. Sometimes other lawyers would also be waiting there. The lawyers would confer and we would wait our turn for our case to be heard by the judge. Sometimes we would be invited into the courtroom for the hearing before the judge, and sometimes we were not. We could never understand the proceedings, as everything was spoken in Arabic. Buhidma would tell us after the hearing what had taken place and what the judge had ruled, but we were never quite sure if we were getting the whole story.

I never saw a woman working in the courthouse. Occasionally, a woman would appear as part of a court proceeding, but most of the people around the courthouse were men. There was one restroom on each floor, but there was no women's restroom. This presented a real problem for Linda because on every day-long visit to the courthouse she would need to make at least one visit to the restroom. If she could not use a restroom at the courthouse, there was no close alternative without returning to the hotel or the consulate's office. I asked our attorney where Linda could go to use the restroom, and he told me that she would have to wait unless she wanted to use the men's room. Buhidma also had little to do with or say directly to Linda. He was Libyan and following Libyan custom he communicated mostly with me.

The restroom was about the size of a large closet, perhaps about five feet square. There was no toilet or wash basin, and of course, no chair. In the center of the floor was a sunken area with a drainpipe about two inches in diameter. There was no screen over the pipe or hole; it looked like a shower drain without the hole cover. On one side was a water faucet and a two-gallon bucket sitting under the faucet. The user was expected to use the bathroom over the hole, then draw a bucket of water and wash it down. Not everyone did a good job, so I always washed down first, before I got close to the hole. I described all of this to Linda before she decided to use the facility. She was understandably reluctant, but decided it was the best of the other options she faced, since she could not wait. She would already look ridiculous coming out of the restroom, and this would be exacerbated by the conservative, but Western way Linda dressed. Arabian men did not try to hide or conceal their interest and curiosity, and would often stare at her wherever we were.

Linda and I walked to the restroom. I checked the room to make sure it was vacant. By this time, three or four men had gathered in the hall nearby, apparently to watch and see if Linda was going to use the restroom. There was no inside lock on the door, and the Arab men freely used the bathroom regardless if anyone else was inside. Privacy was not a concern or an issue for them, but Linda wanted privacy. While she was not normally an assertive person — at least not while on this mission — she let me know in no uncertain terms that she wanted privacy, and I was to see that she had it. My job was to guard the restroom door while she was inside, which was complicated by the fact that the people who used it on a regular basis were accustomed to just walking in without restrictions or concerns, not to mention the fact that I could not speak Arabic and very few of them spoke English.

Linda went inside and I stood in front of the door with my back to the door and my arms crossed. The three or four men watched from about 25 feet down the hall, talking in Arabic. Linda had just entered the restroom and closed the door when another Arab man, robe flowing, came around the corner and walked straight toward me. My fears were realized when he stopped and reached for the door. I was standing in front and said, "No, no," waving my arms. He was puzzled and did not understand. He was speaking Arabic and I did not understand what he was saying, but his tone was not very nice. The men down the hall started laughing. He turned and spoke to them, probably asking what was going on. He looked shocked and backed away to join the other men watching the door and me. Then another man walked up to the door. The restroom had suddenly become a very popular place. I went through the same routine with the second man, but he was insistent on going in. I blocked his entrance a couple of times by holding my hand on the door handle and moving from side to side, like an awkward dance. The men down the hall began bursting with laughter, but I could tell they were not advising the man that there was a woman in the restroom. They were just enjoying the scene. At least someone got enjoyment out of the situation.

While I was blocking the second man, Linda opened the restroom door behind me. The man saw her and was so startled that he almost fainted. He started backing away mumbling and bowing, and I am sure apologizing for his insistence on entering. The watchers continued to laugh and the embarrassed man confronted them. Linda put her nose in the air and her back to the men. She walked swiftly and stiffly back to the waiting room, and I followed her. She said it was awful, and I quickly informed her that it was no picnic guarding the door either. She insisted she would never use that bathroom again, but she did, almost every Sunday for the three months we were there. However, I helped my "guarding" situation by getting our attorney to write out in Arabic on a piece of paper the words, "Woman in Restroom." From then on, when she went to a public restroom, there or anywhere else, I would hold up the sign for anyone who approached. It worked, although it still caused attention and an audience almost every time.

On the day of our second hearing, Buhidma told me that the chief prosecutor, Mr. Ismail Talaat, wanted to meet me. I was informed that he was a powerful figure in the local government. His position would be similar of that to the U.S. Attorney over a district in the United States. I met with him during our long morning wait. He offered me coffee, and I accepted, thus experiencing my first taste of espresso. The coffee was very stout, served in an extremely small cup, with the top part being a very black, muddy-looking liquid. The bottom third was a black mud, too thick to drink; I noticed that some people would lap with their tongue the mud in the bottom of the cup after the top liquid was consumed. I did not like it at all but drank it as a courtesy to my host who offered it, as to decline it would have been an insult to him.

When I went in to see the chief prosecutor, Mr. Talaat, I had no idea why he requested to see me. He spoke very good English and was very cordial. He asked me many questions about my background, my work, and about the Shibley case. I felt I had nothing to lose by laying out all facts and information requested to such a high-ranking and well-placed individual who worked in the same courthouse with the judge and other attorneys. I also took the liberty of telling him a few things that I was sure he wasn't aware of, such as the fact that Sol Shibley had renounced his Islamic faith and worked his way through college by speaking at Christian churches, even though he would quickly endorsed again the Islamic faith as soon as it would benefit him.

Mr. Talaat told me that he had spent several years in the United States. He had a degree from the University of Alabama and had also had military training in the United States. I did not know his true political feelings — even if he felt friendly towards our government, he would be unable to show that in his present position, and I understood that.

I felt I had potential here for an influential contact. Not a friend, necessarily, but someone who might be able to help me in the future, so I took a chance. I asked him if there was anything he would like to have that I could get or do for him. He told me that when he was in the United States, he had seen a particular book published annually by the government on crime statistics in the U.S. I was not only familiar with this book but subscribed to it and had the latest issue in my office.

Titled *Crime in the United States*, it was published each year by the Federal Bureau of Investigations, and I received a new edition every January. In actuality, the contents of the book are public information but very impressive in published format, and this chief prosecutor probably did not know it would be so easy to get, as in Libya, this kind of information about their crime data would probably be secret. I told Mr. Talaat I could probably get him a copy, and I would see what I could do. My next move was to tell Kay or Ronnie on my next contact to send it to me.

At the conclusion of the second hearing that day, we got a jolt of bad news from our lawyer. Buhidma told us that the judge refused to allow the case to go forward unless we could produce an affidavit from the U.S. Attorney General stating that this case had exhausted all appeals in the United States, that custody was awarded to Linda Shibley, and that Sol Shibley had no further right to appeal. The affidavit would have to have an authentication from the attorney general's office. I explained to Buhidma that in the U.S, the attorney general's office had no jurisdiction in this type of case. I pointed out that this was a state case, not a federal case, and the highest court to have jurisdiction was the Arkansas Supreme Court, not the federal court, where the U.S. Attorney General might be involved. Not to mention that Sol Shibley had not even exercised his right to appeal the Jefferson County Chancery Court's decision on the custody award, and that the time for his right to appeal had now expired. The decree I had already provided to the Libyan court was the final decree, and nothing further could be done in the U.S. courts. While I know that this was not the exact truth, I knew the courts back home would not be able to do anything else for us. I asked Buhidma if there was some possible way that we could get the judge to reconsider or to appeal his decision. He said that there was not, that the decision was final and there was nothing that could be done unless I got the document from the office of the U.S. Attorney General. I told him I would let him know what we would do.

Frankly, I thought this was a brush off and a dead end. I believed the Libyan judge intended it to be such. I spoke with Linda about it and explained to her there was almost no possibility of us ever getting such a document from the attorney general's office. She told me we had to try, that her mother had promised to finance us, and she did not want to give up so long as there was the smallest possibility. I told Linda that I did not believe we could turn this task over to anyone else. I knew what had to be done, and while I was not at all sure I could get it, I would stand a better chance than anyone else.

There was something else to consider. Once Linda or I left Libya, I was not sure we would be allowed to return on our visa, because of the anti-American attitude running so high within the government. We agreed that Linda would stay in Libya and I would return to the States to see what I could do. If I succeeded, I would return right away; if I did not, we would confer by phone and assess our options.

Chapter 11

On the Paper Trail

THE NEXT MORNING, we went to the consulate's office and advised them of our plan. Allan Largent, the communications officer, came in and visited with us. He called his wife, then told Linda and me that Linda should check out of the hotel and stay with him and his wife Carolyn while I was gone. He explained that it would be very unsafe for Linda to be alone in the hotel or elsewhere. She would possibly be assaulted, and no Libyan court would take her word over a Libyan male. If she was raped, the Libyan male would say she was a prostitute, and she would be treated as such. Linda agreed to go stay with the Largent family.

I went back to the hotel, picked up Linda, and we checked out of the hotel. After I took her to the Largent home, I drove to the airport, turned in the rental car, and got a one-way ticket to Rome with a plan to get a ticket back home in Rome. My heart was heavy, as I felt there was very little hope that I would be back. I had met the children and felt they would grow up in Libya. Linda would be brokenhearted, and I was not sure she could take that. I flew into Rome that night and the first flight I could get to New York was not until about noon the next day. I stayed at the airport and slept in a chair, but before I went to sleep, l called Kay. I filled her in on what was happening and told her I was coming home.

Kay brought me up to date on what was occurring there at home. She told me that the business was struggling. Ronnie had told her he did not have enough money to pay the bills, take his salary, and give Kay any. I was very surprised to learn that Betty Short, Linda's mother, had not been giving Kay funds on a weekly basis for my fee as she had promised to do. Ms. Short would now owe us about $10,000 in fees and expenses. In order to pay our expenses, I had used my American Express card and had run up about $4,000 on the account. Linda and I had used most of the cash we had with us. She only had her return ticket with her and only a few hundred dollars. Considering where we were in recovering the children, I felt quite uneasy about our finances in the case. We needed the money badly and I was not sure we could do anything more to recover the children.

With all of that on my mind, I boarded an Al Italia flight from Rome to New York. The plane was a new jumbo jet Boeing 747, that carried more than 400 people. This was one of the first 747s in service, and the name on the plane was "Neil Armstrong." The largest plane I had previously been on was a 707, so this was a new experience which, regardless of the circumstances, I cherished.

I flew to New York and flew home as quickly as I could. It was wonderful to be with the kids and with Kay again, but our financial situation was grim, and there were things I had to do for the family, the business, and the Shibley case — for Linda, Kenny, and Nofa. I felt the best chance of helping all was to achieve success in this case.

Early the next morning, I met with Ronnie. I gave him a status report on the Shibley case and received a status report from him on the other work and finances of the business. I reviewed the cases with him and gave him my suggestions, then explained to him I had to give my attention to the Shibley case to see what I could do about meeting the Libyan court's requirements as well as try to get some money from Betty Short.

I left for Pine Bluff, where I first went to see Linda's attorney, Don Smith. I discussed with him the Libyan court requirements and the overall status of the case. His assessment agreed with mine, there was little hope. We decided that I would start with the office of the Arkansas Attorney General and the Arkansas Supreme Court, then go to Washington. D.C.

Don Smith called the office of the Arkansas Attorney General and made an appointment for that afternoon. I already had all documents from the Jefferson County Chancery Court, which were certified, so I felt I did not need anything else from them.

Next, I went to see Betty Short. I gave her a firsthand account of everything I had done to date and told her what I planned to do. Linda had already called her and told her the same thing. She said to me again, "You bring the children home and I'll pay you if I have to sell my home." I told her I would do all I could. I could not promise success, but in order to survive, I had to be paid expenses plus $100 per day. There would be more debt on my American Express with a trip to Washington, and I had about $3,000 in fees due. When Ms. Short gave me a check for $5,000, I was so relieved that I did not press her for more.

I went back to Little Rock and immediately deposited the money. I told Ronnie I had to pay the American Express bill in order to keep working. He was not happy about it, but I insisted. I told Ronnie to use the other business receipts to pay the other business bills. In addition, Ronnie took $400 and I took $600 as personal funds. Kay was terrific about making our funds stretch for herself and our four little children. In addition to the 1969 Plymouth we used as both a family and business car, I owned a beautiful, antique, perfect condition 1946 Chevrolet Fleetline, which we used as a second car. I told Kay that if she got short of money again to sell that car or have Ronnie sell it.

That afternoon, I went to see the Chief Deputy Attorney General of Arkansas, Rodney Parham, Jr. I stressed to him I needed a certified letter stating that the Shibley case was closed, that all opportunities for appeal had passed, and that Linda Shibley had full custody of the children. He studied the certified documents I had and we drafted a letter, then had it typed and certified. I knew this step was easy compared to what I faced in Washington. Parham cautioned me that he did not think I would be able to get such a letter in Washington, but I insisted to him I had to try. I thanked him and left.

After a second night at home with my family and treating them to a dinner, I left for Washington, D.C. on what was viewed as an impossible task by everyone I had spoken with who had knowledge of the law. Anyway, I had to try. I prayed for guidance and gave a lot of thought as to how I could approach the undertaking.

While in Libya, Linda and I had some time to share information about our past and people we knew. One thing she had told me was that while at Ouachita Baptist University, she had a political science professor named Buddy Whitaker who was now employed in Washington, D.C. as a senior aide to Arkansas' senior U.S. Senator, John McClellan. Senator McClellan had been in office over 20 years and was very influential. He was serving as chairman of the committee that oversaw the distribution of funds for foreign aid, as well as other positions. I decided if I could get an audience with Buddy Whitaker and get him on my side, using his old connection with Linda, then perhaps I could approach this from a political angle instead of a legal one. Even though I was not a lawyer, I knew enough about the law to know that from a legal standpoint, I did not have a chance, not even a slim one. So, the political approach was my tactic — if that did not work, I would have to reevaluate.

When I landed in Washington, D.C., I went right to a pay phone in the airport and called information to get the number for Senator McClellan's office.

Mr. Whitaker was unavailable, so I left a message that I needed to see him on a very urgent matter regarding a former student of his, Linda Shibley. I said that she was presently in Libya trying to recover her kidnapped children, and that time was of the essence. I wanted to say enough to get his attention and get an appointment.

I got a cab, went to a hotel, checked in and called the senator's office again. I was given an appointment to see Mr. Whitaker the following morning. I was informed that he had a full schedule that day and the next, but if I would be there at 9:00 a.m. he would try to work me in. I spent the evening going over and over what I would say to Buddy Whitaker. I wrote it out, edited it many times, and rehearsed it over and over. The next morning, I left my hotel about 7:30 a.m., took a cab to the Senate Office Building, and was in Senator McClellan's office shortly after 8:00. I asked them to please tell Mr. Whitaker I was there and would wait until he could see me.

About 9:30, I was called into Mr. Whitaker's office. He told me he did remember Linda as a student and recalled that she had married another student, Sol Shibley. After receiving my message the previous day, he had the senator's Little Rock office research any publicity on the case. There had been several news stories published in the Arkansas papers over the past three months, and the Little Rock office had already sent him a report that morning. He knew that Sol had kidnapped the children, that there was a warrant for him, that I had found Sol in Libya, and I had been there with Linda. I was impressed; he had done his homework, and what he had learned from that homework got me the appointment.

Mr. Whitaker asked me to tell him about the case and how he could help. I assumed my time would be limited, but I gave him a briefing on the highlights of what had occurred and my involvement. I explained to him the ruling of the Libyan court and what they were requiring. Mr. Whitaker was knowledgeable and told me exactly what I suspected, that the judge was probably knowledgeable enough of American law to know he was giving us an impossible task to accomplish and this was an easy way to put up a block that we couldn't overcome. This would cause the case to go away, meaning that the Libyan court would not have to deal with a touchy case that could easily become an emotional international incident. A ruling for Sol Shibley would ignore the American law which had ruled on the case and issued a warrant for him when the Libyan government still wanted U.S. money and help in their oil field exploration and production. A ruling for Linda Shibley would ignore the Libyan, Palestinian, and Islamic laws which held that women had no rights to custody when the father wanted the children. Mr. Whitaker and I both agreed that the Libyan court was simply trying to make the case go away.

I told him that I had to get a letter from the office of the U.S. Attorney General to even have a chance. He told me he did not think I could ever get such a letter, but I asked him to help me get an appointment with someone in the attorney general's office who could give me such a letter if I talked them into it.

Buddy Whitaker then called the attorney general's office and asked to speak with a Mr. Jaffe. Mr. Whitaker told them there was an urgent situation in Libya and that he needed to see Mr. Jaffe right away. He hung up the phone and said, "Let's go."

He told his secretary to either change his other appointments for the rest of the morning or have someone else see them.

Before we left the office, we went to Senator McClellan's office. Mr. Whitaker knocked and entered while I waited outside. He then called me in, and I met Senator McClellan personally. Senator McClellan told me that he understood I had a difficult task, but they would do what they could. The senator asked me to give Ms. Shibley his regards and I thanked him.

Buddy Whitaker had a driver take us to Mr. Jaffe's office. We went in, and they passed a few pleasantries; they obviously knew each other. I learned that Mr. Jaffe was the Chief Civil Attorney for the office of the U.S. Attorney General. Mr. Jaffe heard the story from Buddy Whitaker, who had told me to let him speak until he turned it over to me. Then Buddy turned to me and said, "Fred, you tell Mr. Jaffe what you need." He turned to Mr. Jaffe and said, "The senator and I will appreciate you doing what you can to help. Linda and Fred are constituents of Senator McClellan, and Linda was a student of mine when I taught college. On top of that, what has happened to her is totally wrong. I am returning to my office. Fred, give me a call and keep me posted." I thanked him, we shook hands, and he left.

I then told Mr. Jaffe what the Libyan court required, that I needed a letter from the office of the U.S. Attorney General verifying that the case was final under U.S. law and that no appeals were pending or could be made from this point.

He said, "You know we have no jurisdiction on this case; you have to get this from Arkansas." I told him I already had that and showed him the documentation. I reiterated that without the letter from his office, we were out of court entirely. I told him there was no assurance we would win even then, but without the letter from him, we could not even get a hearing, and the children would be left there.

I also told him there was already a lot of publicity on the case, and Buddy Whitaker had assured me he would do what he could to help. I knew I was stretching what Buddy Whitaker had said, but I felt I had nothing to lose. I was playing hardball with my comments, but if I walked out without the letter, we were done.

Finally, Mr. Jaffe called in his secretary and said to me, "You dictate a letter like you need. She will type it up and I'll look at it." After working with the secretary, this is what we drafted:

UNITED STATES DEPARTMENT OF JUSTICE

WASHINGTON, D.C. 20530

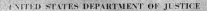

A F F I D A V I T

I, IRVING JAFFE, Deputy Assistant Attorney General
of the Civil Division of the Department of Justice of
the United States of America, hereby state that the en-
closed pleadings, decree and order of the Chancery Court
of Jefferson County, Arkansas, are properly certified by
the Clerk and the Judge of that Court and that the decree
of divorce which provides among other things for the
custody of the minor children to be placed with the
Plaintiff, Linda Faye Shibley, is, within our Court
system, a final decree and as such is entitled to and
would be accorded full faith and credit in the various
states of the United States of America.

IRVING JAFFE
Deputy Assistant Attorney General
Civil Division
Department of Justice

For   JOHN N. MITCHELL
Attorney General of the United
States of America

Sworn to before me this
___27th day of August, 1970

___Notary Public

Mr. Jaffe looked at the letter and signed it, along with three copies. I was so grateful; I was almost moved to tears. When he handed me all the copies, I took a copy from the bottom and handled it across the desk, telling him, "Here is your copy." He said, "I don't want a copy. As far as I am concerned, I have never seen this letter." We shook hands, I thanked him, and I left.

I borrowed a phone outside and called Buddy Whitaker. I told him I had the letter I needed, and he congratulated me. Then I told him I had to get the seal of the U.S. Department of State on it in order to take it back to the court in Libya and get it filed.

Mr. Whitaker told me to meet him outside. I went out and waited at the curb, and a short time later, Mr. Whitaker arrived in a staff car. I got in and we went to the State Department. We went in, and Mr. Whitaker explained what I needed. They assured him they would do it, and he told me he had to go, but for me to keep his office advised on the progress of the case. I thanked him, assured him I would, and he left. After the State Department authenticated the letter, I took a cab back to my hotel, checked out, and went to the airport. I found I could get a plane home at 6:00 p.m and be home by about 10:30. I called Kay. I was ecstatic, and she was subdued. She was glad I had been successful in getting the letter but was afraid for me to return to Libya. I had some concerns also, but felt I had no choice. I told her to stay home with the kids and ask Ronnie to pick me up at the airport. When I arrived in Little Rock; Kay was at the airport. She had a sitter with the kids. We both knew that in a couple of days, I would be gone again, and we wanted to make the most of our time.

The next morning, I called Betty Short, told her I had gotten what the Libya court required, and would be leaving the next day to return to Libya. I told her I needed additional funds to keep going on the case. She tried to put me off, but I insisted, and said I would come down to discuss it. I prepared a status interim billing at the office and took it to her. My time and expenses showed that she still owed me over $3,000, and the bill continued to grow every day. I told her that if she would give me $3,000 now to catch up, then give to the business $1,000 a week to apply towards expenses and fees until we returned, that would suffice. She agreed, and I brought another $3,000 back home with me. I gave most of that to Ronnie and told him to save at least $1,500 to put on the next American Express bill. I took about $1,000 for my expenses but gave Kay about $200 of that before I left. This left only about $500 for other business expenses, but Ronnie had receivables coming in from other work to use.

I spent that night with the family. We got in the car and drove to Warren to visit my mother. She, too, was anxious. We did not stay long, just had a brief supper and then returned home. I made flight reservations to leave the next morning for Libya and purchased the round trip ticket with my American Express card.

I sent a Western Union telegram to Linda, in care of Allan Largent at the U.S. consulate's office, saying that I had the letter needed to get another hearing, and telling her when I would arrive in Benghazi.

Before leaving Little Rock, I remembered the book of crime statistics that the chief prosecutor, Mr. Talaat, had said he would like to have. I packed my current copy in my suitcase and took it back with me, so I could give it to him at the first opportunity. I flew through New York, to Portugal, Paris, and then on to Benghazi. I was back in Benghazi about ten days after I had left, with the letter which the Libyan court required in hand.

While I was away, I sent an assortment of letters, telegrams, and postcards to Kay. The image below is the Benghazi Palace Hotel where we stayed while awaiting the court's decision

Chapter 12

Back to Libya

ALLAN LARGENT MET ME at the airport, and we went to his house, where we celebrated the fact that I had been able to get the letter. Allan and Linda told me we had an offer that could provide some financial relief for us, in terms of saving on expenses. One of the major oil companies owned a large house in a nice area of Benghazi that they used as a guest house, usually allowing executives and guests to stay there temporarily while in Benghazi. Because so few guests were visiting at the time, they had spare rooms. Linda had been staying with the Largents while I was gone, and we stayed there that night with them. The next morning Allan drove me to the car rental agency, where I again rented a Volkswagen Beetle. He called the oil company office for me, and then Linda and I went by to talk with them about our staying at their guest house. They refused to accept any pay and gave us keys and a map so we could find it.

We returned to the Largents' home, got our luggage, and using the map, went to find the guest house. We found it to be a very large, three-story house. There was only one other guest there. We selected a couple of bedrooms and moved our luggage in. We checked out the kitchen and agreed to go grocery shopping after we visited with our local attorney.

We headed to Buhidma's office, where we met with him and I showed him the letter I had obtained. He was obviously very surprised that I had been able to get the letter as required by the Libyan court. We discussed it, and he told me that I would have to get it translated by the court-approved translator, bring it back to him, and he would file it with the court and ask for a new hearing. We immediately went to the translator's office. He agreed to translate the letter by the next day, and we paid him in advance Our objective now was to get the case re-filed with the letter required by the court and get a decision as soon as possible on whether the court would honor the child custody order from Arkansas or not. Our attorney, Buhidma, was not optimistic, but we were taking it one step at a time.

We then went grocery shopping so we could eat at the guest house and save money on food.

We got the groceries and went back to the guest house, where Linda made dinner for us. We had a visitor that evening, who came unannounced. It was the oil company official I had met at the reception given at the consular officer's home right after our arrival in Benghazi. The man — we will call him Mr. Smith — worked for the company which owned the house, and he asked about our comfort with the house. We thanked him for the room and board and offered him a Pepsi as you could not get Coke in Libya.

Mr. Smith asked me to go for a walk. He suggested he and I walk around and to take a look at the property. I suspected he had something he wanted to discuss away from Linda, but also was concerned that the house was bugged. He asked again about my experience and abilities as a pilot, a subject he had been interested in when we first met. We again discussed planes I had experience flying, as well as asking about our case, the children, and what we thought our chances were of succeeding. I told him that our lawyer was not optimistic, but we were going to give it our best shot. We hoped to be successful, but if we were not, we would then look at any other options we might have.

He pointed out the property next door and told me about it and the history of the guest house. Smith then got to his real point.

He told me he would offer a possible option for us if I was interested, but it would have to be kept between us. I told him that any other option was good news to me. He said that if I wanted to consider flying the children out myself, he could make a Cessna 180 available for me. The Cessna 180 is a very nice four-passenger high wing durable plane able to take off and land on short runway, as well as cruise at over 160 miles per hour. I told him I was *extremely* interested. He said he could have the plane available at an isolated landing strip near Benghazi, one used by the oil company. It would be topped off with fuel and ready to fly, and the keys would be in it along with air maps, charts, navigational aids, et cetera.

There is an island, Sicily, about two-thirds of the way across the Mediterranean headed towards Italy, that was within the range of the 180's ability. If I could navigate it, the plane would get us there. All I would have to do would be to get Linda and the kids to the plane, which would be a daunting task, since Linda was not allowed to take the kids out alone. Then I would have to fly out under radar — staying down to 200 feet above the ground — get out over the water as quickly as possible, and fly basically on the water, probably at about 100 feet above the water. I told him I could handle the flying, but the harder task would be to get the kids to the plane.

Smith gave me a phone number I could call to get a message to him and told me he would need two to four hours' time in order to have the plane available for me. I was amazed that he had made such an offer, let alone that he was being this generous. He did tell me that after the plane was taken, that he would have to take the official position that the plane had been taken without their permission. I later realized that this was probably an offer that would benefit his company as well as it would be a way to get one of their planes out of Libya, which they would otherwise lose to the Libyan government when the oil company property was seized. Smith then got in his vehicle and left.

I later told Linda about his offer. Like me, she was amazed that such an offer had been made. The Americans there were supportive and helping us any way they could. They understood the problems and the options.

The next day, we picked up the translated letter and took it to Linda's attorney, who assured us that he would get it filed with the court right away.

We began a series of weekly hearings every Sunday. The cost of staying there in Libya was a strain so I used my American Express card to cover many expenses. Betty Short, Linda's mother, did not send the $1,000 a week to Kay or Ronnie as promised. Ronnie was, of course, supposed to be working other cases, bringing in money. Our other investigator, Mel Fry, was also supposed to be working and generating income. Kay helped some at the office along with caring for our home and our four small children. I was hoping the business would be self-supporting plus allowing Ronnie and Kay to each take a salary while l worked on the Shibley case. The business had been doing well before I left, but when I got home, I learned the business had lost money while I was away, and both Kay and Ronnie were almost desperate for money. Kay kept this from me as much as she could while I was away, but I had started to get the drift before the Shibley case was over.

At a hearing in late September, about three weeks after I returned to Libya, we were told that the next hearing would be three weeks away, around Oct. 20. Our attorney said we could do nothing for the case until then. They had all the evidence and the judge would simply make a ruling.

It occurred to me that we might go home for two weeks and then come back. I considered the cost of roundtrip tickets for Linda and me versus the benefits. My main benefit would be two weeks spent with my family, which meant I could work on other cases at home and earn money there as well as try to work on the finances of this case with Betty Short. Linda mentioned to me that her mother, Ms. Short, had told her that her church in Pine Bluff wanted to have a fundraiser to help support our efforts financially. She told me that if the fundraiser took place, all the funds raised would go to help cover our expenses. Things between Ms. Short and I by now were strained because of broken promises, but I knew I could not give up my efforts on this case. I had to see it to conclusion, even though the prospect for a positive outcome looked bleak. I had to know that I had done all I could.

I wrote down all the pros and cons of going home versus waiting in Libya. On the pro side of returning to the U.S. was the fact that our lawyers had advised us to go. We would have no trouble from Sol if we were out of the country and would have some relief from the sheer tension of just our day-to-day existence there in Benghazi. There was not much difference between the cost of roundtrip tickets and the cost of staying in Libya, and back home, I could earn some money on other cases, while publicity might help us raise funds to support the costs of the case. On the other hand, if we left, it meant Linda missing her brief weekly visits with Kenny and Nofa.

With all of this in mind, I laid out a plan to Linda. We would go home for two weeks. She could help prepare for the fundraiser and hold it just before we returned to Libya. I would help some for publicity to raise interest. We would then return to Libya and see the case through. We agreed, so with my American Express card, I bought us round trip tickets home. We left Benghazi on Oct. 2 and came home for a little over two weeks, returning to Libya around Oct. 18.

Before leaving Libya, I found an opportunity to deliver the book on crime statistics to Mr. Talaat. He was so proud to get it, thanked me profusely, and told me, "I'll remember this gift." To him, it was a treasure, and the small effort of bringing him this book later paid very big dividends for me.

We notified Kay and Betty Short that we were coming home for two weeks. We went and visited the children before leaving, and then flew home. It was so good to see my family again but we did a lot of work to try and improve our financial situation. While home, I was invited to be a guest on a Channel 7 television show, along with Linda. She plugged the fundraiser that her pastor and church were organizing.

There were a couple of favorable news articles which also helped. I worked every day in our business on local cases, went to see clients, generated new cases, and did all I could do to help improve our financial situation. I spent every evening, night and Sunday with my family. We also visited our relatives and they visited us. It was a busy and wonderful two weeks.

The second Saturday we were home, the Calvary Baptist Church on 17th Street in Pine Bluff hosted a fundraiser from 10:00 a.m. to 5:00 p.m. The local radio station, which had given a lot of publicity to this story, set up a live continuing broadcast from the church for seven hours. Once an hour, Linda and I were interviewed. Judge Dawson, who had handled the case, came by and was interviewed along with the Pine Bluff mayor and other political government officials, members of Linda's family, including her mother and grandmother.

Many people made contributions, though I do not recall the total amount collected. The church administered the funds, and I think it was almost $10,000. My firm, Myers, Rand & Associates, was paid about $5,000, of which about $3,000 went to pay my American Express bill for our round trip home and other expenses. That helped but I still had never billed any fee since going to Libya, only expenses, and I had not been paid any fee for my time. Betty Short never kept her promise to send to Kay or to our business the $1,000 per week she had agreed to send toward paying the additional funds we were owed.

Chapter 13

The Final Challenge

ON OCT. 17, 1970, we flew back to Libya for our next hearing, which we hoped would bring success to our mission: to recover the children. I was concerned about going back, however. The Libyan government was rapidly becoming more hostile to Americans. However, they were still receiving money from the United States for oil exploration and development in exchange for the promise to continue to sell oil to the United States.

The connection we had established with the office of Senator John McClellan was invaluable. He was chairman of the committee that oversaw the distribution of funds overseas to foreign governments for such matters as oil exploration. Every week, he sent a telegram to the American ambassador in Libya, asking the status of the Shibley children's case. The ambassador would then, on behalf of Senator McClellan, make an inquiry of the Libyan government who, in turn, would make an inquiry to the court officials. The message soon became clear: very important people in the U.S. government had a keen interest in this case.

I will never know exactly how much influence this had, but I expect it was extremely beneficial in several instances. For example, when we landed in Rome, we were scheduled to depart on the next flight of the Libyan National Airlines to Benghazi. As we were boarding the plane, the security personnel pulled me out of line, took me back inside the terminal to a private room, and turned me over to three Libyan security agents. I was strip-searched, including body cavities, which was the only time that has ever happened to me, and it was a rather humbling and humiliating experience. They questioned me about my business in Libya and noted from my passport that this was my third trip to Libya in three months. They made calls — I suspect to Libya — to check out my business there. Suddenly, they told me to get dressed and stuffed my things back into my bag; there was a sudden change in their attitude. When they first pulled me from the line, I quickly told Linda to go on, even if I did not come back, and to report it to the consular officer as soon as she got to Benghazi. She seemed very relieved to see me come aboard the plane.

We touched down in Benghazi that night and went to our hotel, since the guest house was no longer available. The next morning, we went to the hearing, but the only thing that came from that hearing was the news that another hearing would be held on Oct. 30, over a week away. We were told this would be the final hearing, where a decision would be made. Arrangements were made for Linda to visit the children, and I went with her.

The next day, the consular officer called me at the hotel and asked me to come to his office right away, so I went immediately. He told me that the U.S. ambassador, Joseph Palmer, wanted a meeting with me right away in Tripoli. The best travel option would be to fly, but when I went to the airport to buy a ticket, I was refused a ticket to travel from one Libyan city to another. So I rented a car.

The next morning Linda and I left for Tripoli. The road was small, a two-lane black top with a lot of potholes and herds of wild camels along the road. We carried water and sandwiches, stopping only for gas and the restroom. There were a lot of trucks on the road. We drove straight to Tripoli, arriving very late at night. We checked into the same hotel we had stayed at three months earlier when we first came to Libya.

The following morning, we went to the U.S. Embassy. After we identified ourselves, we were shown to Ambassador Palmer's waiting area. He came out and met us and visited with both of us, asking about our case and the children as well as about our families back home. He then asked if Linda would like a tour while he and I visited. She accepted, and he invited me into his office.

Once we were alone in the office, he offered me a chair and then got right to the subject he wanted to discuss. He told me I did not have to tell him anything, just listen to him.

Ambassador Palmer said he had heard a story that if we were not granted custody of the children that we had a plan to spirit the children to a stashed single-engine plane and fly them out of the country. The ambassador quickly assured me that he was not asking if this plan was true, but if it was, I should consider certain things. He said he understood that if the Libyan courts did not return the children to Linda, there was almost no way we would get them later, considering Libyan law. However, he warned me that attempting to fly out of Libya in a small single-engine plane would be very dangerous. He understood that I would be flying low, on the water and under radar, but no doubt the Libyan military would scramble and try to find me. If they did, I would not have a chance. If we were caught and survived, we would be jailed for a very long time. American authorities could not intervene, because I would be charged with violations of Libyan law. He warned me that the consequences could be very severe and tragic. He suggested that we rethink this plan, but again assured me he would not interfere or reveal anything about our plan to anyone. He then changed the subject until Linda returned from her tour. He wished us well and said goodbye.

It was about noon when we left the embassy. We decided to depart for Benghazi immediately, because Linda wanted to get back so she could try to visit the children again before the next hearing. We departed as soon as we stopped for gas and snacks.

There was a small town about the midway point, which is where we had gassed up on the way from Benghazi. We drove about 300 miles, getting to the small town about 9:00 p.m. The gas station was closed, and there was no way we could continue without gas. No one spoke English, it was dark, and the men stood around and stared at us. We felt like they were vultures, waiting to pounce on us at the first opportunity. I drove around the small town and spotted what appeared to be a small motel. We checked into our rooms, which were next to each other. Each small room had two cots, and there was a community bath for the whole floor off the hallway. We agreed on both of us staying in one room, and one would sleep while the other sat near the door with a light on and the door cracked open. That way, we each got about four hours of restless sleep that night and we could communicate with anyone in the hallway.

We prepared to leave early the next morning. For Linda to use the restroom, we just about had a repeat performance of the incident at the courthouse a couple of months earlier. We left at the first break of daylight and drove to the service station next to the highway for gas. I filled the car as soon as possible, and we left without washing our face or brushing our teeth. We were just glad to be back on the road.

We had time while driving to discuss and consider what the ambassador had told us. I knew the risk was remarkably high if we attempted to escape with the children, but I did not have the heart to rule it out. I knew that if we were not successful in court, there was little chance of Linda getting the children back unless we took them by force. However, if we failed, I might never see my family again. I was very stressed. Linda was at least able to visit her children for four hours, knowing it might be her last visit.

We went to court on the morning of Oct. 30 for the final hearing. Our attorney asked us to sit quietly. All conversation was in Arabic, so we could not understand. Sol Shibley was there with his attorneys. Armed military and police were around, but that was not unusual; they were always around.

The lawyers went to the front. We had a new judge this morning, not the same one who had been there for the previous hearings. There was a long conference before the bench. The armed police and military were called to the front and the judge spoke with them. Then Sol Shibley was called to the front. After a few brief statements from the judge, Sol Shibley became highly agitated. He raised his voice, speaking in Arabic and waving his arms around. I was astounded when the armed police and military pointed their weapons at him, to which quickly quieted him down.

Our attorney walked back to Linda and me and told us, "The judge awarded the children to you, Mrs. Shibley. They are in the hallway with a caretaker and you may take them and leave."

I turned and said to Linda, "Let's go."

The lawyer cut me off quickly and replied, "Mr. Myers, you are not free to go. You must report to the chief prosecutor." I felt a pit in my stomach. I told Linda to take the children and go to the hotel. If I was not back in a couple of hours that she was to take the first plane home with the children. The attorney offered to drive her to the hotel, and I was escorted to the Office of the Chief Prosecutor by the police.

When we arrived at Mr. Talaat's office, he greeted me and told the police they could go. He told me that the court had awarded the children to Linda Shibley, an amazing ruling, as it was not consistent with Libyan law. The ruling in our favor was no doubt due to political pressure and was probably why there was a new judge on the case. He told me that while Linda and the children were free to leave Libya, I was not free to leave and, in fact, I was to surrender my passport to him.

I felt if I surrendered my passport, I would be in Libya for a very long time. I carried my passport in my sock on the bottom of my foot, and to protect myself, I lied. I told Mr. Talaat that my passport was back at the hotel and I needed to go get it. To my amazement, he agreed to let me go get my passport alone. I did not expect that, but when he told me that, I immediately felt that he was giving me an opportunity to get away. He knew when I walked out, I would not be back freely.

I shook hands with him and told him, tongue-in-cheek, that I would get my passport and bring it to him later that day. I left and drove to the hotel. I walked into the room where Linda was and motioned to her not to talk. I wrote a note, "We are leaving now. Get your things." I had parked the vehicle near the back. I walked down to the desk while Linda packed, and told the desk I would pay our bill up, but I did not check out. I paid up to date and then went back upstairs. We got our suitcases and walked down the back stairs, three flights. We put everything in the car and drove to the consulate's office. We explained to the consulate's office what had occurred, and they congratulated us and told us we were very fortunate.

The consular officer took me aside and told me that I might be prevented from leaving, and I asked for his advice. He told me there were two flights leaving that night. The first, to Rome, would leave about 5:00 p.m, and the second, to Athens, Greece, would leave about 8:00. He told me that if I tried to leave along

I sent the good news home by telegram right away.

with Linda and the children, and there was a "hold" on me, they might hold all of us.

There was another complication as well. The children's passports had not been issued and new vaccination records had to be obtained in order to get said passports. It was too late to get those records that day, but the consular officer offered to help and said that the records could be completed the next morning. Linda and the children would then be able to leave that day. I would be gone and there should be no problem with Linda and the children departing for Athens.

The consular officer told me that if I planned to leave first, on the 5:00 flight to Rome, the airport and the airline might not yet have a "hold" on me in their system and that I might be able to get through. The longer I waited, however, the greater the risk of my being held by airport officials and not allowed to leave Libya.

Linda asked me to stay and leave with her and the children the next day, but the consular officer advised me to leave as quickly as I could. By the next day, I might not be able to leave. He assured Linda that he could take care of the children's records and passports, and that either he or Allan Largent would accompany her until everything was done. They would take her and the children to the airport and see them safely off.

I felt that I owed it to my family not to take any unnecessary risks. There was very little risk of Linda and the children not being able to leave once the consular officer completed the paperwork for the children's passports. Linda already had the court order allowing them to leave, so they should not be stopped if I were not with them. I told her I had to go.

The consular officer called the airline and made reservations for Linda and the children to leave the next day for Athens, then on to New York and home. The tickets were paid using my American Express card, which he then returned to me. We then drove by the residence of Allan and Carolyn Largent, who fed us a quick supper and we discussed our plans with them. I said goodbye to Carolyn, Linda, and the children.

The kids and Linda gave me a hug, and Linda said, "Thanks. I'll see you in New York."

I drove the rental car to the airport, where I went up to the counter and paid the bill up plus three extra days. Allan Largent drove his car to the airport and hung out to make sure he would know whether I was able to get on the plane and depart, or if I ran into any problems.

I did not try to buy my ticket right away. Instead, I made myself scarce, out of sight, in a public restroom, where I changed into different clothes. The plane was to depart at 5:00, so I waited until about 4:15 before going to the ticket counter, really pushing my luck to get a ticket.

I got in the ticket counter line and when I got to the window, I kept it as simple as possible. I had my visa and passport ready, and I bought only a one-way ticket from Benghazi to Rome, so there would be no complicated scheduling. There would be plenty of time to arrange the rest of my journey home once I was safely out of Libya. I spent as little time as possible with the agent.

It worked! I do not believe the agent checked for my name on his list of prohibited flyers because if he had, I might never would have come home. I got my one-way ticket to Rome, checked my luggage, and again, tried to get lost in the crowd. When the plane was ready to board, I boarded as quickly as possible. I simply sat quietly and prayed under my breath. All I wanted to do now was get off the ground in this plane and go home to my family.

My prayers were answered. After what seemed to be a very long time, the plane taxied out and took off. I said a prayer of thanks as we lifted off the ground. For the first time, I felt I had a good chance of getting home within a couple of days, even though I was still on board a Libyan Arab National Airlines plane. I even allowed myself to think about the huge check Betty Short would gratefully give me upon my arrival home in a grateful gesture of appreciation to me for laying it all on the line in order to recover her two grandchildren and bring them home. I was daydreaming, of course.

The plane ride across the Mediterranean to Rome was uneventful, but I stayed awake and alert. I was even more relieved when we touched down in Rome. As I disembarked from the Libyan National Airlines plane and walked into the terminal in Rome, I knew then I was finally free from the reaches of the Libyan government.

I was convinced then — and am still convinced — that I was allowed to leave by the chief prosecutor because he did not believe in the actions of the Libyan government. Mr. Talaat understood and agreed with me and what I was doing in Libya, and he knew if I did not get out then, I would probably never make it out.

I immediately retrieved my bags, went to the Al Italia Airlines ticket counter, and bought my ticket for the first flight to New York. During my wait for the plane, I called Kay and updated her on the day's fast-moving events. I told her that Linda and the children and I planned to meet in New York so we could fly home together. Kay agreed with that plan, provided I didn't get held up. I told her I would keep her as updated as possible.

Kay filled me in on a very important event that was taking place at home. We had rented a small two-bedroom house for the past year, and we were crowded. Kay was looking around for a bigger place but, until now, our finances had been very limited. Kay told me she had found the ideal home for us. It was only about three blocks from our present home and only

$75 more than our present monthly rent. I felt the bigger, better home was the least I could do for her after all she had done the past few months, so I said okay. Kay is and always has been a very supportive wife, and I am thankful for that.

I boarded the first Al Italia flight to New York and slept most of the way. Upon my arrival in New York, I went to a phone and called Betty Short. That was the first I learned that Linda had changed the plan. We had agreed that she would call her mother as soon as possible with her schedule and we would try to meet at the New York airport. However, Ms. Short told me Linda was in Athens, and had decided to stay there for a couple of days to spend time with the children.

I told Ms. Short that I would fly home and would meet the plane in Little Rock when Linda and the children arrived. I checked flights to Little Rock and got an American Airlines flight out that afternoon. I boarded and flew home.

I looked forward to returning to a normal life, and most of all, to having my family around me and sharing life together. I got home late that night.

Nofa and Kenny Show Some Toys They Got in Benghazi to Mrs. Shibley and Myers

Photo from the Pine Bluff Commercial, Nov. 8, 1970

Chapter 14

Home Again

KAY HAD ARRANGED a lease purchase agreement on our new home and moved in with help from friends and relatives over the past few days. My first night home we spent the night in the home that would be our home for more than 20 years.

The next morning, I went to the office and first met with Ronnie to review the business and where we were on work. Ronnie seemed stressed with the business, and relieved that I was back to help him. We still had one investigator, Mel Fry. We were doing our own office and secretarial work without a secretary. Ronnie and I organized the work and planned what each would do.

I checked again with Betty Short for Linda's planned arrival home and she told me Linda would be home about noon the next day. Ms. Short told me a large welcome party had been arranged to meet the plane at the Little Rock Airport. Persons who would be there included the mayor of Pine Bluff, Governor Rockefeller's administrative assistant and Bozo the Clown from Channel 7. There would be live television coverage, and a welcome party of 50 to 100 people.

My first task was to put together and detail my invoice to Betty Short. I had kept her advised as we worked the case, and she had paid our firm expense reimbursements from time to time. However, no complete accounting had been done, and I had not billed for any time since I left for Libya in July. I had kept financial records, but they had to be detailed and put forth in a proper invoice. While I was working on the invoice, I received a call from Buddy Whitaker. I thanked him profusely for his help. He told me that Senator McClellan had decided to fly to Little Rock early the next morning and would be in town to accompany me to the airport to meet Linda and the children. I was asked to pick him up on his arrival, take him to his hotel, then pick him up again on my way to the airport to meet Linda and the children. I was delighted, of course, because I could thank him personally.

I worked most of the rest of the day on the billing between phone calls from people, relatives, clients, and friends who were just touching base with me. My figures showed I had spent a little over $25,000 of my funds on expenses, in addition to what Linda had spent herself. I and my company had been reimbursed about $22,000 in total, including that paid to Ronnie and Kay by Betty Short while I was in Libya. I was still owed about $3,000 in expenses, plus my fee. Before leaving in July, I had agreed on a fee of $100 per day. I had been on the case a little over 100 days — totaling to $10,000 in fees for my work, plus the remaining expenses of about $3,000 not yet reimbursed, for a total balance of a little over $13,000.

The next day was Monday, Nov. 2, 1970. That morning, I picked up Senator McClellan, dropped him at his hotel, and arranged to pick him up again about noon to go meet the plane with Linda and the children. Kay, Ellen, Lee, Katy and Christie were also driving out to meet us to welcome them home. We were all at the airport at least 15 minutes before the plane arrived. It was a great welcome home party. The news media interviewed several people, including Senator McClellan,

The children's homecoming brought out the press and many local dignitaries. Above: In front, Betty Short holds her granddaughter Nofa, Linda Shibley stands behind her son Kenny. At left is U.S. Senator John McClellan. At right, just over Linda's shoulder, is Pine Bluff Mayor Austin Franks. Below: Even Bozo the Clown turned out to welcome Kenny and Nofa home.

Bozo the Clown, and me. The plane arrived, and it was a joyous time of hugs and tears, especially between Kenny, Nofa, and their grandmother.

Linda hugged and thanked me, then departed for Pine Bluff with her family. Kay and our children returned home. I drove Senator McClellan back to his hotel, thanked him again, and assured him that I was well aware that without his influence, the judge most likely would not have made the decision to return Kenny and Nofa to Linda on Oct. 30. We shook hands and I went back to work.

The almost six months that I spent on the Shibley case were some of the most challenging and harrowing of my career, but even now — nearly five decades later — I still consider that case the crown jewel of my years as a private investigator.

* * *

Ironically, after all the excitement of the children's return, their overjoyed grandmother, Betty Short, said nothing further about paying me.

I plunged back into my work and other cases. Ronnie told me that he would like to leave the firm and seek employment elsewhere. We had formed the partnership of Myers, Rand & Associates several months before, with great expectations and dreams. I believe the pressures of the Shibley case, taking me away from my family for most of three and one-half months, as well as the financial and personal pressures generated as a result, were just too much. Ronnie was newly married and making that adjustment, and the business required long hours, hard work, and dedication. I respected his decision to leave. When we formed the company, we did so on a shoestring and started with only a few hundred dollars I loaned the company. I told Ronnie that if he was sure he wanted to leave, I would take over the company, which had no assets except a few receivables, and owed current bills. I would continue his salary for three months while he found other work and adjusted financially, and I would assume all company debts. He agreed, and we parted on friendly terms. Mel Fry, our investigator, stayed with us. I then hired a secretary to replace Ronnie, planning to do most of the field work myself with Mel Fry's assistance.

Meanwhile, Kay was planning a large party in our "new" home, as a combination housewarming and a celebration for our concluding this case. We wanted to invite Linda, so I called her, and she accepted the invitation. After a visit on the phone, I told her I had sent my invoice to her mother, with a copy to her, and asked if her mom had mentioned when she would pay the bill. Linda suggested I call her mother and discuss it with her.

For the first time, I wondered not only when I would get paid, but if I would get paid at all. It was hard for me to accept the fact that I had done what I had done on her promise, and she might not come through. I knew enough about her to know she had the funds and would not have to sell her home to pay me. I called Mrs. Short and told her I really needed the funds and would like to drive down to Pine Bluff and pick up my check, as she had received my invoice a week or so earlier. She told me to come down and discuss it, and we set an appointment.

A few days later, I went to Ms. Short's residence. The main purpose was the talk about payment of the $13,000 owed to me. No one mentioned that the first half hour. Finally, I told her I would get back too Little Rock if she gave me my check. She said she had discussed it with "Short," her husband, and they would pay me the $3,000 for the rest of my expenses, but someone else would have to pay my fee. I reminded her of our agreement and her promise. She never denied it, but simply stated while handing me the check, that she could not pay me any more than that. I remained calm and simply stated that I had to be paid, and that I needed it badly. I really could not believe or accept the fact that not only had I risked my life but that my family had endured over three months of hardship and our business had almost collapsed. There were few people who would have or could have done what I did for them, and now they were reneging on their promise to pay me.

Linda was a teacher and had no savings, only her salary and two children to support. But her mother had the money to pay and had promised to pay. I made the difficult decision not to pursue the debt legally. Although my business needed the money I was rightfully owed, I did not want a lawsuit to tarnish the successful outcome of this challenging case.

* * *

In the decades since our return from Libya, I have seen and visited with Linda from time to time, but as the years have passed, we have had less and less contact. Linda retired from teaching and moved out of state. Sol Shibley stayed in Libya for many years, but Linda told me he later returned to the United States.

Chapter 15

Onward

THE SUCCESSFUL RETRIEVAL of the Shibley children marked a turning point in my career. Although the case was a disappointment financially, its aftermath put my business on the map in a whole new way.

After our return from Libya, there was a lot of publicity and several news articles, all raving about our trek to rescue the children. I was invited to speak at many Bar association meetings and other gatherings, such as the Optimist Club and the Lions Club. *Redbook* magazine offered to send a reporter from New York to interview me and write a story; however, I declined their offer.

Nevertheless, due in part to the publicity, my investigative business flourished. I became well known in the legal community and started getting a lot of missing persons cases, making me the leading missing persons private investigator of my part in the nation for roughly the next 20 years. My growing popularity lead me to investigations that would take me overseas multiple times — to places as varied as Egypt, Canada, Venezuela, and Mexico.

I decided to build up the business by offering other services, such as a courier service for law firms and security services.

Private detective, Warren native working on complicated child custody case

It's the end of an exacting ordeal
Shibley children back from Libya

'It's Over,' Says Teacher Who Journeyed to Libya To Find Her 2 Children

Father Has Custody Again

Shibley Custody Trial Is Postponed
Mother Continues Recovery Efforts

A Long Ordeal
Linda Shibley, Nofa, Kenny Are Home From Libya

ARKANSAS GAZETTE, Thurs., Sept. ...

Decision Expected Oct. 4 By Libyan Court in Case On Custody of Children

Gazette
TUESDAY, NOVEMBER 3, 1970.

... State News Service
of the two children of
who were spirited aw
now is in the hand
in the international
day from Libya w

Pine Bluff youths are held in Libya; custody in question

**** Thursday, September 17, 1970 ARKANSAS DEMOCRAT

Libyan judge to rule on suit to return 2 children to mo

Governor Intervenes in Shibley Case

Happy Homecoming for Mrs. Shibley
Mrs. Shibley greets her mother, who is holding Nofa Jane in her arms while her son Kenneth stands between them.

I became active in several professional associations and took advantage of their professional development resources. I began to be called upon to testify as an expert witness in depositions and at trial, in Arkansas and elsewhere. In over 20 years, my testimony was never impeached.

In 1971, I co-founded the Arkansas Private Investigators Association, serving two terms as president. In my role as chair of the legislative committee, I helped to draft proposed legislation to regulate private investigators and security personnel in our state. I testified before the state legislature to help get the bill passed in 1977. My business continued growing alongside my roster of clients — many of whom would become national figures.

Through the years, our business has gone through changes. Sometimes I have worked in partnership with others, and at other times it has been strictly a family affair. Each of the children has worked with the firm at one time or another. Today, my son Andy carries on the family legacy as the owner and manager of Attorney's Services Inc. He is a licensed private investigator and court-appointed process server.

Even though I enjoyed my professional role as a private investigator, my favorite role is father and grandfather. One of the great joys of Kay's and my life has been watching our family flourish and grow as our children have married and presented us with grandchildren. Our first grandson, Jordan Ryan Reed, was born to Christie and her husband Jay in May 1994, and our first granddaughter, Emily Katherine "EmKay" Myers, was born to Lee and his wife Tracy 12 days later. Two years later EmKay's baby brother, Andrew Land "Drew" Myers was born. In September 1996, my daughter, Katy, married her husband Todd, and his son Taylor became our fourth grandchild. Katy and Todd's daughter, Katherine Copeland "KC" Nicholalds, was born in January 2000. My son Andy and his wife Stephanie brought us three more grandchildren: Teagan, Tony Lee, and Trinity. We have taken great delight in each member of our growing family and all of our family's adventures.

As I look back over the years, I can see how my life has been shaped by every experience I have had and every choice I have made. Sometimes I have taken a step back, sometimes even a step sideways, but I have always kept my faith and my family as my fundamental values. I have been blessed with a rich and fulfilling life, and I still look forward to every new adventure with my family, with intuition by my side — and a passport in my shoe.

With my son Andy Myers, then an aspiring detective, now my successor in the business, doing some on-the-job training near the border of Mexico.

Volume II Preview

Detective Fred Myers went on to handle more than 2,000 additional private investigation cases, including several other child abduction cases which took him to various foreign countries in order to solve the cases and recover the children. Below is an excerpt from the next book.

Since moving to Little Rock in 1969, our investigative business had continued to grow, working routine investigations including insurance disability cases and missing persons cases. In the winter of 1981, it happened again. The phone rang and, as fate would have it, my secretary was away from her desk and I answered the call. When Mary Lee Orsini called me that day and requested that I check on the questionable activities of her husband, I never would have expected that call would become another big case.

The details of the final report on the Orsini case are as chilling as any private detective could ever imagine being given the responsibility to investigate. That one phone call led down a road of twists and turns, deceit and manipulation, and the deaths of Mary Lee Orsini's husband and her attorney's wife.

www.ExpertPress.net

Made in the USA
Coppell, TX
28 January 2021